CAREGIVER'S GUIDE

Getting Started, Making It Work, and Finishing Well

CAREGIVER'S GUIDE

Getting Started, Making It Work, and Finishing Well

Linda Kloth

PUBLISHING

© 2018 Linda Kloth

Caregiver's Guide: Getting Started, Making It Work, and Finishing Well

Published by Azure Seas Publishing
www.azureseaspublishing.com
Seaside, CA 93955
Printed in the United States of America

All Scripture quotations are taken from the Holy Bible, New International Version®, NIV®. Copyright © 1973, 1978, 1984, 2011 by Biblica, Inc.™ Used by permission of Zondervan. All rights reserved worldwide. www.zondervan.com The "NIV" and "New International Version" are trademarks registered in the United States Patent and Trademark Office by Biblica, Inc.™

ISBN 978-1-950058-22-8 (softcover)
ISBN 978-1-950058-21-1 (ebook)

Library of Congress Control Number: 2020912939

Cover photo courtesy of Pixabay.com.

To Grandma and Grandpa Kloth

Table of Contents

Preface

Many caregiving books and programs focus on the caregiver—what it means to be a caregiver and how to take care of ourselves. Or, they inform us about dementia, but leave us with questions. This book helps you get started with caregiving and shows how to negotiate the fine points and intangibles of helping a loved one finish well. It addresses practical points and questions:

- When should I help? How do I know they need help?
- Where can I turn for help as it's all beginning and I'm trying to figure things out? What do I need to consider? What are the options? Where do I start?
- What can I do when it's time for my parent to stop driving? This effects independence and daily life.
- How do we preserve respect and dignity when our elders can't make all their own decisions anymore?
- How can we help our elders have the best quality of life when they cannot live alone anymore?
- How to keep sane and do well as a caregiver. What if I don't want to do it? How to avoid falling into abusive patterns.
- The fine line between helping someone vs. helping someone stay as independent as possible. How independence relates to dignity and respect.

- Logistics such as medication and allergy lists, dealing with power of attorney, and how to avoid predators and scams.

How This Book Was Born

I saw gradual changes during the first five years living with my grandparents, with significant changes the years that followed. In time it became evident that Grandpa and Grandma could not live alone.

They got confused over the mail. Even though the medical EOB (explanation of benefits) states "This is not a bill" they worry that it is and wonder if they need to send money in. They have spent an hour debating this one matter, and still not sure what to do, they sent a check in for fear of missing a payment.

When a phone call comes in with an automated message, they can't understand or follow it, so they don't know if the call is important. For example, when they receive an automated call from a pharmacy that their prescription is ready, they can't catch which pharmacy is calling or who the prescription is for. They can't even write down the number or identify the caller or type of call. Life is not easy.

They sometimes get very confused or frustrated when they can't interact in today's world. That frustration can last all day. I've heard my grandparents talk seemingly forever about things they can't resolve or understand. If they didn't have someone to negotiate or translate their experience in today's world, they would live in confusion and frustration, and make big mistakes (financially, medically, logistically).

They are prone to scams. I have helped them avoid multiple phone scams, remove computer viruses, and stop pushy strangers from entering the home to show off some product.

It's not only about avoiding problems. I play card games with them—a highlight in their day. I make dinners they enjoy. I go shopping for things they want and help them find obscure things online.

One Day in the Life

A sample of one day: bring in the newspaper, plan dinner with Grandma, answer the phone, put Grandpa's contact lens in his eye, wrap his right ankle with an ace bandage, bring in the breakfast food from the outside refrigerator, bring in the lunch food, help Grandma find more honey in the cupboards, bake muffins.

Gram and I discussed solutions to Grandpa's bowel problems, including which kinds of medicines and supplements are appropriate. I brought the basket of laundry in for Grandma. I brought the mail inside. At midnight, they called on me to help Grandpa remove his contact lens.

The day before, I set up the big Christmas decorations and placed the boxes of small decorations in a place Grandma can easily reach. If I wasn't here, the only thing they would ask a neighbor to help with is retrieving Christmas boxes from the rafters. Some of these things they can do by themselves. Yet the risk of injury is higher, since they are not as balanced, coordinated, or dexterous as they used to be, and their vision is limited.

That's why I stayed to the end. It's a fantastic privilege. I invite you to join me for an inside look, as we consider together when to step in, how to step in, and how to help one another in this wild, wonderful, and sometimes wacky life.

A note to the reader: this book was written while my grandparents were alive. That keeps this record of caregiving alive and relevant. Though they have both said goodbye to this world, it seems best to keep the written account of our stories in present-tense.

Chapter 1

Motivations

"Don't ever grow old." —*Grandpa Ed said this*
often after he turned 90

Everyday People

The hunched-over woman crossing the busy main
street with her walker. The frail elderly man slowly
making his way around the grocery store by himself.
A woman whose eyes don't see above the steering
wheel, driving home at 20 mph as cars race dan-
gerously around her. An elderly couple, walking
gingerly, entering the doctor's office together.

I see them everywhere I look, elderly people with
no one to help, trying to make it through life. I'm not
talking about all "senior citizens." This is not about
people of any particular age. It's about people who
have lived to a ripe old age, whatever age that happens to be, who now need help. For many, there is
no one there to help.

My heart goes out to them. I wonder who will take them to see the doctor. Who takes them to get their prescriptions filled or makes sure they know how to use a new medication? How do they get groceries, clean the house, take out the trash? Do they tell someone if they are having chest pains, or just hope the pain will go away? Who sits with them at night so they don't feel lonely? Who sees that they need help?

When the family comes to visit, do these elders put on their best face and pretend for two days that they can still manage alone? I am a stranger on the street. Yet I see many people trying to navigate life past the time they are able to manage on their own.

I see my own grandparents, who do so much, yet can't do it all. I see them trying hard when people visit them. Everyone wants to believe that they are fine. So do I.

Yet I also see and hear the things we don't want to see and hear. I hear when Grandpa falls in the shower, not once, but four times in one month. I see when Grandma gets Grandpa's medications mixed up, giving him two antibiotic pills a day instead of four. I am with them in the doctor's office, so I know that they forget important things the doctor says, or even get the doctor's words all mixed up. Like the time Grandma came back from the eye doctor saying that she doesn't have macular degeneration, when in fact she did.

Aside from needing someone to physically drive them from place to place, my grandparents need help to continue living safely and healthily at home.

The Pattern

When they were in their 50s and 60s, my paternal grandparents went to live with his mother for ten years. They originally intended to bring her 300 miles away to their home, but she was determined to stay in her own home.

When she had passed away and they moved back in their own home, they cared for Grandma's sister many years. Edna lived in a care home (as it was called) only two miles away. They visited her several times a week and organized activities at the home.

My maternal grandmother, Grandma Laura, and her sister, Aunt Margaret, lived in an apartment directly next to the convalescent hospital that housed their mother. They visited her every day for many years until she left this earth.

Later, when Grandma Laura's apartment was destroyed in an earthquake, she went to live with my parents, who cared for her until she went to heaven.

I have grown up with great examples of caring for aging family members. So, while I sometimes struggle with the challenges of living with my grandparents (let me be honest: "challenges" means those severely frustrating days when I want to bang my head against the wall), I don't struggle with the question of whether or not to care for them.

The Alternative to Living at Home

Several years ago, Grandma and I visited two of her friends, at two different "care" institutions. First we visited Nina, who was in convalescent care following surgery that required a long recovery. At the front entrance, we wove our way past many people in wheelchairs. They had long faces and empty eyes, hungry for love and attention. All of them sat in chairs, facing the door, waiting for something—life?

We walked down the halls. Someone who could not get out of bed called out from their room, "Help me! Someone help me!" No nurses were running to help.

Out of other rooms we heard moaning, crying, and TVs blaring. It was a nightmare.

Then we reached Nina's room. She was happy and proud to have visitors. But she was honest with us.

"I hate it here! I want to go home!" she exclaimed. Then she cried loudly.

Gram and I did our best to encourage her.

Next we went to visit Olivia. She was also in a facility for long-term recovery, recovering from a fall.

This dignified woman sat quietly at her bed, the curtain drawn between her and the roommate for some privacy. Her roommate had the TV on constantly. Olivia forced a smile, but I could see that it was not a great situation. She admitted that there was not much to do. She sat there most of the day with nothing to do and no friends to talk with. She seemed to do better than the other patients though, who also called out for help from their rooms or shuffled slowly down the hall with blank stares.

As a sensitive person, it affected me deeply. I determined that no matter what the cost, I'd do my best to keep my grandparents from having to live in a facility. Deep inside I determined to keep them from ending life like that. Even if they have to be in a home, they will not be left alone.

They gave us an example of caring for family and taking care of each other, without ever talking to us about it. In fact, even though they acknowledge their need for help, they talk more about not causing an inconvenience to anyone. They don't want anyone to go out of their way to provide help.

Accidental Caregiver

I landed at my grandparents' home in California, seemingly by chance. I stopped by to visit on my way to San Francisco, where I'd planned to get a new job and make a new start. But I got stuck in Seaside. One weekend ultimately turned into years.

During that time, it became evident that Grandpa and Grandma needed some help with daily living. At that time Grandpa was still driving and Grandma was still making dinner every night.

Those of us who lived with them helped with various things from time to time. Mitch replaced their broken refrigerator. Danny painted the eaves. I helped with various things that came up.

Slowly through the years the level of help needed changed. At the start, they needed help from time to time to keep things going smoothly. Five years later, they need help just to make daily life at home possible. It didn't change overnight, although it does for some people, such as when a stroke strikes or a fall breaks the hip.

Importance of Presence

If there were no family members here to help—to paint the eaves around the roof or drive them to the grocery store each week—they likely would have been in a serious accident or had a serious unaddressed medical problem.

According to the Alzheimer's Association (one of the best resources available for those suffering with dementia):

> People with Alzheimer's and other dementias who live alone are exposed to higher risks—including inadequate self-care, malnutrition, untreated medical conditions, falls, wandering from home unattended and accidental deaths—compared to those who do not live alone. An estimated 800,000 individuals with Alzheimer's (or one in seven) live alone.[1]

There is no doubt that Grandpa and Grandma's longevity was extended and well-being preserved by the presence of caring family members in the home. I can't count the number of times I have happened upon them when they were in the middle of a dangerous task or about to begin one.

One day when I walked into the backyard I noticed Grandpa bending over a garbage can, digging things out of it, and transferring them to another can. I wondered if I should help, but decided not to bother him, respecting his independence.

Two minutes later I walked back out. This time he was leaning against the fence. He couldn't move. He couldn't walk. Something was wrong but we didn't know what.

I pulled a chair over for him to sit on, then searched the garage for a wheelchair. He didn't want that. Yet he still couldn't walk. After he sat a long time, I helped him walk slowly to the house. He is a big, heavy guy. It wasn't easy.

Of course, he didn't want to see a doctor. Refused to go! The next day, He was in enough pain to agree to go to a chiropractor. Turns out he had partially dislocated his hip!

These kinds of things happen too often. Every one or two months, something unexpected happened, requiring professional attention. Yet on a weekly and bi-weekly basis, mishaps are prevented by our presence.

I have concerns for other elders I see in daily life around us, who are living alone. First and most importantly, their health is at risk when they don't have help. Anyone can fall and not have someone around to help. It may sound silly, but really, if someone has broken a hip, they can't crawl to a phone to get help. Common problems may be less serious, but people often don't get medical attention when they need it.

Whether it is lifting heavy things, falling, having a stroke or a heart attack—something is likely to happen sometime. The question is, will someone be there to help at that time?

I was talking with an uncle about these things, and the importance of being around to help Grandpa and Grandma. My uncle was advocating greater independence for them. He didn't want Grandpa and Grandma to need help yet. I totally understand. Even with me here, accidents and things still happen. I can't stop an accident or health emergency. What I can do is be here to help if it happens. And my help prevents some accidents before they have a chance to happen. A live-in caregiver prevents a number of accidents from ever happening.

What is the point or significance of preventative care? We are all going to die sometime, right?

There are very clear and specific benefits from preventing accidents and minimizing the risk of such accidents.

Life for Grandpa would be awful if he broke his leg and had to be laid up in bed for months. Of course, he wouldn't stay in bed. So his leg wouldn't heal and he'd end up in a convalescent or rehab facility. Would he like that? Who would pay? Who would manage the house while he is there? (All of the bills, the utilities, the yard, the food sitting in the refrigerator, his mail, etc.)

Our quality of life is better when we aren't laid up. Many people stuck in a bed all day in a long-term institution become depressed and lose motivation for life. That's not to say there is no quality for those who are stuck in bed or in a care facility. Life is what we make of it. But it sure is a lot harder on a person.

Speaking of quality of life, that is another benefit to being here with my grandparents. Not only do I get to help them live together at home, I help them have a better quality of life than they would have without someone around to help.

That's how I ended up an accidental caregiver. It also explains why I stayed, even though some people encouraged me to "get on with life." I want to help my grandparents finish life well and I'm willing to make some personal sacrifices to help them do that. It is sometimes difficult and frustrating. It is also very rewarding.

There is not always a sign in the road or an email message in the inbox telling us, "Your parents need a lot more help." Or, "Without help, your mom isn't succeeding with daily life." We often have to discover that on our own. The next chapter gives some tips for seeing the signs along the road.

Chapter 2

When Do I Get Involved?

And those who were seen dancing were thought to be insane by those who could not hear the music.
—*Friedrich Nietzsche*

When the music changes, so does the dance.
—*African proverb*

The Dance

It is a delicate dance when that time comes. Whether the aging loved one is a parent, grandparent, spouse, aunt, uncle, close family friend, or long-time neighbor—it can be anyone we know and care about—the level of involvement differs for everyone.

Having helpers can be the difference between getting regular meals, paying bills on time, keeping utilities on, safety around the house, and more. By being available, our family helped my grandparents avoid scams, get out of scams they fell into, remember what the doctor said, and take a medication properly.

The stories and anecdotes included here center around my experience with my grandparents with the hope that, though your situation is unique, our story will reflect situations you may face.

Signs It's Time

Now that I'm over 40, I sometimes find it harder to read signs from far away on the highway. I hate to admit that, but it's true. It's easier when I'm watching for a specific sign, like the name of an exit. It's that way when helping loved ones. If we are moving too fast and don't know what to watch for, we may speed by without seeing the sign that says, "It's time to help." So what are some signs to look for? Let's get straight to it!

The Yard Isn't Kept Up

It's not hard to figure this one out. Just look at the yard and compare it to the level that you are used to seeing. Is the yard work getting done or is the grass unkempt and the weeds overtaking? It's also common for people to do yard work, then spend the rest of the week recovering in pain. The poker tell for hidden pain is not wanting to get out of the chair or move around.

It's not a crime to have an overgrown yard and not a crime to not feel up to doing yard work. It's a sign of physical limitations for many. An unsightly yard can be a point of frustration for someone who's used to keeping it up. It's a big blessing to step in and care for the yard, or hire someone to help with it. It may be a sign that the time to pitch in with more help is coming soon.

Difficulty Cleaning House

Like yard maintenance, this is an easy sign to spot, unless you are just visiting for the weekend. (If it's a weekend visit, it's almost guaranteed that the house was well scrubbed before you arrived.) There are many reasons a house may not be clean. When an unclean house is related to the aging process or a sign of needing help, it may be due to loss of vision, lack of motivation or depression, or more aches and pains that cause physical limitations.

My grandma always kept a clean house. Not spotless, but clean. Then crumbs began to appear on the floor. Crumbs scattered across the kitchen counters. Shelves in the house loaded up with dust. Grandma's eye sight was diminishing. She didn't see the dust and crumbs, so she didn't clean. Not to mention that her body just wouldn't allow her to keep the house up to former standards.

When a house can't be cleaned over time, it can become an unpleasant or unhealthy place to live or visit. It's got to be kept up and cleaned at some regular intervals. Those of us who live long enough may find a time when we don't have enough cartilage in our elbows and knees to do it all on our own. Not everyone likes someone else to clean their house, relative or not. So it may take some negotiating, but don't be afraid to get proactive at this point.

Difficulty Managing Meals

This big sign is also difficult to spot on a weekend visit, especially if you treat your loved one to dinner or help out in the kitchen. It's very normal to eat less at meals as we get older. I know some people who skip meals, especially lunch, and it's okay. It can also be challenging to find meals that agree with an aging and changing digestive system, so it's important to be sensitive to that when we prepare meals for someone else.

If you visit from out of town for more than a weekend, don't take over meals. Rather, observe how meals are handled, if they are skipped, or if preparation is a burden.

There are many options for solving challenges with cooking at home. Your main job is to spot any challenge, help provide a solution that your loved one is comfortable with, and follow-up to see that it's successful.

Grandma was never one to be ready on time. Time management isn't her gift. Food is her gift. She loves baking, cooking, and making others gain weight! So when meal times began getting later and later, I knew something wasn't right. She would be in the kitchen for three hours getting supper ready. We sometimes sat down after eight o'clock at night with growling stomachs. Then I knew it was time to step in and help with meals, even though she still reigned as queen of the kitchen.

That was the start. After being a kitchen helper for three years, she actually asked me to start cooking all of the dinners for us. I was surprised. I'd never suggested it. It was a big change for her, because she had lived most of her life in the kitchen. Yet, she felt she didn't have the energy for it anymore.

If I wasn't there, she would be wearing herself out every night fixing a meal for Grandpa. And they would be eating at erratic hours.

Can't Manage the Remote Control
Let's face it, cable TV providers give out remote controls with about 50 small buttons and tiny symbols and print. All it takes to get confused is switching cable providers once, or buying a new TV or device. At some point when we get older, it's best to keep the same device and not switch, because it's too hard to learn a new system. Sometimes there is no choice, and that can be hard to deal with.

If your loved one can't do things they used to be able to do, such as find the channel they want to watch, they probably also need help in more areas of daily living.

My grandparents enjoy watching their favorite TV shows. Grandpa watches baseball and football. Grandma records "The Price Is Right" and "Wheel of Fortune" so she can watch them at the end of each night. Grandpa was The Man, because he could call up the shows from the VCR and fast forward through the commercials. After a while, VCRs were no more and theirs broke. Then digital TV ushered in the cable box, with a new remote.

Grandpa has been extremely frustrated because he can't learn to use the new remote. He never had problems in the past. Now, he just can't get it. At his request, I created step-by-step illustrated instructions on how to use the remote to get to show recordings. He still can't work it. (That's

Alzheimer's disease at work, not just the normal aging process.)

It's one thing to have difficulty with electronics in general, or with a new device, or with a complex function (such as setting up a weekly recording). It's another problem altogether when normal daily activities can no longer be done.

Trouble Paying the Bills

Maybe this happens because someone is broke, maybe not. Either way, watch for this sign. Money is tricky business, and requires a lot of trust. It's a sign to watch for. Unfortunately, if there's a problem, you may not know until a utility is shut off, or the house is foreclosed, or someone is turned out of the apartment. You get the picture.

One day Grandpa was upset because the electric bill was twice as much as normal. "Guess how much our electric bill is," he told me, "Six hundred dollars!" When I looked at it, I discovered that three hundred was carried over from the previous unpaid bill. After that happened several more times, I knew it was time to step in and help more with the bills. I wasn't sure how to do it initially, while respecting his independence and dignity, since he didn't want help.

One day I noticed that Grandpa had sat at the table for five hours staring at the checkbook and bills. I walked over and asked, "How's it going?" He made a disgruntled sound and told me he was working on paying the bills. It had never taken him that long before and he looked confused.

That is not a sign of normal aging. That is a sign of dementia or Alzheimer's disease. For a quick reference, see "10 Signs and Symptoms of Alzheimer's" at the end of the book. Certainly, it's a scary thing to think of. But it's more scary to avoid the issue out of fear of it.

Whether it's due to Alzheimer's or just general difficulty managing this complex life, your loved one may need help paying bills and managing the bank account. If a utility is shut off or you discover credit issues, it's time to step in, so they don't get in serious trouble.

There are several creative ways to monitor things like this. For example, the gas and electric company in our area, has a free service so children of seniors can be notified before service is shut off due to unpaid bills. What a great way to make sure our parents aren't sitting in the dark!

Auto Accident, Getting Lost, Difficulty Finding Places
We all get in accidents. It doesn't mean we are elderly or in need of care. However, if your elder loved one is having difficulty with these things, it's worth taking a closer look. Driving is such a huge issue, the next chapter is solely dedicated to it.

Difficulty Understanding the Changing World
This took place in a variety of ways. I saw much of it as I spent time with them on a daily basis. If I were only visiting them for the weekend and one of these problems came up, I would probably have considered it a rare mishap. I would've helped them

solve the problem, without considering that more problems may be showing up. Things like:

- Can't find the phone number for a business. Frustrated that the phone book doesn't have the information they want. (Most of this information is on the internet these days.)

- Grandma's favorite food seasoning is no longer sold at the store. (This happens often at Costco, where some products are launched for a limited time before going mainstream.) Grandpa drives her to three different grocery stores, but still can't find it. I can find it for her online.

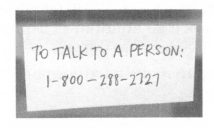

This sticky note was on Grandpa's desk.

- Frustration that when they call a business, they have to listen to recordings instead of talk with people. This happens frequently when they have questions about medical prescriptions or trouble with the internet and cable connection.

- Grandpa doesn't understand why he can't withdraw money from his savings account more than three times per quarter without paying a fee.

- Can't find something in the house. This happens too frequently. Since I have been around for years, I remember that Grandma threw out that cracked vase two years ago when she was cleaning the garage. She doesn't remember. She assumes that it's been misplaced and that we should keep searching for it. (This usually leads to one of those "I want to pull my hair out" moments.)

Whatever the case may be, the world is rapidly changing. When I'm 80-something, I will be dismayed when I can no longer make purchases with cash. (That day is right around the corner!) Further down the road, I will not be able to keep up with the latest technologies and I'll need friends and family to help me do things that every young person can do with ease.

My parents, who are in their sixties, had me set up their internet banking and online bill paying services. They need occasional help with today's technology, but they can still live independently, adapting and living with relative smoothness in today's world.

Your loved one may be experiencing challenges on any part of the spectrum, from needing occasional help, to needing regular assistance, to help with daily living. In any case, it's good to watch for clues that signal greater involvement is needed. The longer we live, and the faster the world changes, the more likely that time will come for the elders in our lives. I saw all this happening first-hand over time with my grandparents as an insider living in their home.

Changing World

The world is always changing, and we aren't always changing with it. I remember the day Grandpa was asked not to write checks anymore for his purchases at the store. Writing checks used to be his way to pay for almost everything. That's how he grew up paying for things.

As much as we talked about it on the way home, he never really understood why they didn't want checks anymore. It's not that Grandpa is unintelligent. At 75 years old, he learned to use a computer!

As intelligent and resourceful as he is, Grandpa's mind wasn't able to process new information as well after a certain point. For him, it began when he approached 90. There is no magic age. It's different for everyone.

Many people I know who have aging parents, when they tell me what's happening and wonder what to do, should already be stepping in, but aren't. The reasons to step in and be involved? To help your loved one finish well by increasing quality of life, removing barriers for them to accomplish goals, and potentially minimize dangerous situations that could bring harm.

Dementia vs. Normal Slow Down

Be aware of the role of Alzheimer's and dementia in aging. Growing older and needing help doesn't automatically mean someone has Alzheimer's or any other dementia. However, the genes we inherit, the lifestyle we live, along with longevity and other factors may influence the likelihood of dementia. Don't let fear or denial keep you from being informed.

Did you know that Alzheimer's patients are usually 3–5 years into the disease before it's identified? Know the signs and symptoms. Increased forgetfulness is only one sign. Poor judgment, physical coordination problems, and withdrawal from social activities are other signs.

Dementia is not a specific disease. It's an overall term that describes a group of symptoms associated with a decline in memory or other thinking skills severe enough to reduce a person's ability to perform everyday activities. Alzheimer's disease accounts for 60 to 80 percent of cases.

—*https://www.alz.org/alzheimers-dementia/*
what-is-dementia

Why be aware? Early use of medication can slow down the onset and disease progression, advance planning significantly reduces stress on families, proper diagnosis will aid in receiving benefits, and logistical challenges can be resolved in advance.

After attending a free class at my local Alzheimer's Association, I realized that my grandparents had signs of dementia. (See "10 Signs and Symptoms of Alzheimer's" at the book's end.) It explained some of the mysteries and helped me become a better carer.

Learning to recognize the signs of Alzheimer's disease is just as important as learning to spot a stroke and heart attack. I also learned those signs, so I can respond quickly and appropriately if Grandpa or Grandma have one.

An Outside Look In

I saw what happened when others came to visit my grandparents. We all do it to some extent: put on a bit of a show, try to look like we have our act together. This is often twice as true for our elders. Some of them are well aware that they aren't making it. They are also aware and afraid that if a relative sees it, they may be forced to move and give up their independence. While that is not the case for everyone, it's a reality for many.

Grandpa and Grandma always put on their best face when people come over. Grandma stands a little taller when people come to visit. Grandpa is more jovial and gruff all at the same time. People who don't live with us don't know what's normal behavior and what's not. It takes more than a weekend visit to spot the signs.

Honestly, it's like a mini-miracle happens when we have visitors: Grandpa and Grandma act very normal with very few mishaps or odd happenings. If something odd does occur, it appeared to visitors as abnormal, rather than common. After the visitors leave, life returns to normal, with all the daily challenges that we've become accustomed to.

Tips for Visits

If you are only able to visit your parents or loved one for a holiday two or three times a year, how can you know the real situation?

First, observe carefully. When something odd happens, inquire about it. If you know your loved one, you probably already know if they're inclined to make a small issue big or a big issue small.

Chat with the neighbors. If they are aware that things have been growing increasingly difficult, they usually want to pass on the news.

If a neighbor goes out of their way to contact you or tell you that things are not all right, listen carefully! You just received valuable inside information that it's time to help your loved one.

Try to schedule a visit for a week, or even longer. You'll get a much bigger picture of what daily life is like, such as whether shopping trips are smooth or challenging.

Know the Signs, Make the Call

Now you know the signs to watch for and dementia is on your radar. If everything checks out and your loved one is going strong, it doesn't hurt to simply ask if they'd like help with something. Maybe they would like help with a bigger project, like painting the house. (In which case, you'd probably rather not ask!)

Are there signs it's time for your loved one to get care on a monthly, weekly, or daily basis? Daily doesn't necessarily mean 24 hours a day. It may be only an hour or two each day at the start. The level of help or care needed at the start depends on when you start noticing the signs.

Apart from a true emergency, there is rarely a single moment that says "daily help is now necessary." If it doesn't happen in a "suddenly moment," as with a broken hip or stroke, it happens gradually over time.

After a few years living with my grandparents, life starting to get more difficult for them. They needed occasional help. As time has rolled on, the level of need grew. It would've grown with or without me here.

Whether you or a family member is there for an elder on a daily or occasional basis, the issue of driving is best addressed as early as possible. One of the biggest challenges we faced was whether or not to interfere when Grandpa's ability to drive became questionable. Understanding the driving dilemma is critical to a smooth transition down the road.

Quick Check List

- ❑ Yard up to regular standard
- ❑ House up to regular level of clean
- ❑ Loved one is not chair-bound due to pain
- ❑ Eating regular meals
- ❑ Meal preparation is smooth and habitual
- ❑ No visible problems with driving or transportation
- ❑ No new dents or scratches on vehicle
- ❑ Can go shopping without unusual stress
- ❑ Able to manage everyday life
- ❑ Using electronics like remote control without difficulty
- ❑ All utilities are working
- ❑ No envelopes arriving marked "overdue" or "urgent"
- ❑ Neighbors don't mention any concerns

Chapter 3

Driving Changes Everything

The one thing that unites all human beings, regardless of age, gender, religion, economic status, or ethnic background, is that, deep down inside, we all believe that we are above-average drivers. —*Dave Barry,* Dave Barry Turns Fifty

You know, somebody actually complimented me on my driving today. They left a little note on the windscreen. It said "Parking Fine."
—*Tommy Cooper*

Yikes!

One of the biggest family challenges came when Grandpa needed to stop driving. Driving equals freedom! Personally, I love to drive. I can't imagine giving it up. Grandpa couldn't either.

It was a true battle to get him to stop. His eyesight wasn't the biggest problem, though he'd lost vision in his right eye due to macular degeneration. His slow response time and growing lack of coordination posed greater danger.

I remember when I first felt fear riding in the minivan with him. We were making a two-hour commute to the Stanford Medical Center near San Francisco. Grandpa didn't seem to notice, react, or care as he frequently hit the lane divider bumps.

"You know what those bumps in the road are for?" he asked. "They help blind people drive." I wasn't laughing.

All the family tried to discourage him from driving. Others offered to drive, but Grandpa refused. It got so bad that when we knew he was planning to drive somewhere, we hurried to get the keys, with hope that he would let someone else do the driving. That plan totally back-fired one day when he refused to let me drive. He was so angry that I wouldn't give him the keys, he came around the van to physically take them from me. He is a big man, so I dropped the keys and ran.

His sons told him it was time to quit. His wife told him again and again. He heard stories on the news about advanced-age drivers plowing into people at bus stops. Nothing could convince him.

We placed hope in the DMV. We hoped that when his license had to be renewed at age 89, they would test him. No such luck! He was able to renew by mail.

I looked online and found that the California DMV offered a form for reporting drivers that should no longer be driving. I thought I'd found a solution. I told other family members about the option of reporting to the DMV, hoping someone else would step up. No one did it, even though everyone agreed he should not be driving. He would be an angry man if he was forced to stop. If the DMV suddenly revoked his license, he would be on a mission to find out who reported him. No one wanted to be that person.

I agonized over the decision for a long time. I feared that if the DMV took Grandpa's license, he would become depressed. Depression was a legitimate fear. Yet it stood in stark reality to the safety of others, especially innocent drivers, cyclists, and pedestrians. "Fatal crash rates rise sharply after a driver has reached the age of 70."[2] There were no easy answers. There was only the obvious fact that he needed to stop driving.

Finally, it got to the point where I wouldn't ride with him when he drove. Grandma soon followed suit. It was difficult to endure his angry outbursts as we held our ground.

Our refusal to ride with him is probably what finally moved him to let others do the driving, although there was no final word or discussion about it, no day to point to and say, "That's when he stopped."

Whatever the scenario, when driving stops, things change. In fact, the change can be so major that it's often the turning point in the role of the carer, and simultaneously begins to threaten independence. That blow to independence, plus the sheer logistic challenge of daily life without driving, are the very reasons many folks resist the call to cease driving, even when they know it's time.

Every family, every person has a different experience. This chapter will address ways to make the transition smoother as driving abilities diminish.

What Changes When Driving Stops?

Once Grandpa stopped driving, it meant he and Gram needed someone to drive for:

- Grocery shopping (average two per week)
- Doctor appointments (average three per week)
- Clothes shopping and shopping for specialty items (Gram likes craft and sewing shops)
- The bank for cash withdrawals and deposits (Grandpa didn't want to use the ATM)
- Church on Sundays
- Eating out at restaurants

They became dependent on me and others who could drive them. For the first time in ages, they had to ask someone to get where they wanted to go. They couldn't go out alone anymore. (They would never consider calling a taxi.)

It created an additional role for me and tied me to the house. Going away for a week wasn't an option unless someone else could be there to drive them.

When I started driving, Grandpa stopped going to church with Grandma. He never liked going to begin with, but he went so he could drive her there and home. It saddened Grandma when he stopped, even though she didn't want him to drive.

Over time, it also meant that I became Grandma's primary shopping companion instead of Grandpa. Not being Grandma's official driver took away one of his major roles in her life.

It's difficult to foresee all of the consequences to come when our loved one stops being mobile through driving. No one wants these things to happen. Yet, when driving becomes dangerous, change must happen.

Signs It May Be Time to Stop Driving

How do we know it's time? Here are specific signs to look for:[3]

- Do they get lost on routes that should be familiar?
- Have you noticed new dents, scratches, or other damage to the vehicle?
- Have they been warned by a police officer about poor driving performance, or received a ticket for a driving violation?
- Have they experienced a near miss or crash recently?
- Has the doctor advised them to limit or stop driving due to a health reason?
- Are they overwhelmed by signs, signals, road markings, and everything else they need to focus on when driving?
- Do they take any medication that might affect the capacity to drive safely?
- Do they stop inappropriately or drive too slowly, preventing the safe flow of traffic?
- Do they suffer from dementia, Alzheimer's disease, Parkinson's disease, glaucoma, cataracts, arthritis, diabetes, or other illnesses that may affect driving skills?

Additional signs to watch for:

- Driving too slow or fast for the situation
- Not staying in lines, difficulty making turns
- Slow response time, poor choices, near misses
- Missing traffic signals and signs
- Other drivers honk often
- Unable to find a familiar location
- Late coming back from a routine trip
- Keeping a foot over the brake pedal
- Confusion and anger with driving
- Confusing the brake and gas pedals (In this case it's time to stop driving.)

Most state laws require that certain health changes be reported to the DMV. We are obliged to follow these laws for everyone's safety. Now we know the signs to watch for and when to act. The next question is, how do I tell someone it's time to stop driving?

The Discussion

Not all end-of-driving scenarios need to be difficult and painful. Grandma quit on her own when she felt that her vision was no longer good enough. Thank God! In fact, the best scenario is when someone concludes for themselves that it's time to stop driving—or change driving patterns—rather than having someone else tell them.

One of the best ways to prepare our loved ones (and inadvertently ourselves) to know when it's time to stop driving is talking about it before it's time. It's wise to have discussions about driving along the way. For those who have the opportunity, now is the time to tackle this touchy subject.

Even if you anticipate opposition to the discussion, it's better to start early, because it will only get harder the longer you wait. Discussing it before it's actually time keeps much of the sting and urgency out of the discussion. We humans tend to fight change. When we have time to think about and consider changes without pressure, we are more likely to be ready when the time comes.

Here is the big, hairy goal: respect the independence and dignity of the person you speak with, while keeping public safety a top priority. Plus, find viable solutions to living, and maintaining independence and social life when driving stops.

Starting the conversation can be direct or indirect. Being direct may include a question like, "Have you considered that there may come a day when you can't drive anymore?" An indirect discussion may begin with a story about someone else you know who had to stop driving.

Ask your elder or spouse how they feel they are doing with driving, if they think there may come a day when they will need to stop driving, and how they feel about it. From there, you'll want the discussion to include signs it's time to stop or modify driving patterns.

Discussion points for an early talk about driving:

- Open the discussion
- Talk about signs that it's time for someone to stop driving (included in this chapter)
- Will they will decide when to stop or do they want input from others?
- Discuss making modified or gradual changes as an early option for safety
- How they feel about the situation?
- What kind of transportation options would they consider when driving is no longer an option?

If It's Time to Stop Now

If you haven't had a chance for advanced discussions, and the time to stop driving has come, or needs to be seriously considered, the discussion will differ. Oftentimes the discussion can be depressing or discouraging for our loved one. They may feel angry about the situation—more about the situation than the fact that you brought it up, so don't take it personally even if that anger appears directed at you.

Some doctors will help when medical factors require a person to stop driving. Getting an outside expert to advise can be helpful. However, most adults prefer to hear from their adult children about driving. It's also helpful if you've personally ridden in the car while they were driving, so you can give specific feedback and factual observations. Don't let initial negative conversations prevent you from addressing the issue again.

Most adults prefer to hear from their
adult children about driving.

Gradual Change

Not all situations require a complete moratorium on driving. Our abilities often change gradually, so we can adjust as those changes take place. The key is watching for and recognizing the time to start adjusting.

Types of gradual changes that help:

- Avoid night driving, especially if bright lights interfere with vision or if signs and routes are difficult to perceive.
- Avoid driving in heavy traffic hours to reduce stress and odds of an accident.
- Don't drive in bad weather. Rain and snow especially reduce visibility and safe road conditions.
- Reconsider difficult routes, such as ones that include busy highways or difficult left turns.
- Do stick with familiar and shorter routes.
- Do go to classes that teach senior drivers how to stay safe on the road.

Alternatives to Driving

Once it's time to stop, the next step is finding viable solutions to transportation needs. Several options exist.

The Future

Soon driverless cars will be readily available. Some are already on the road and have proven to be safe.[4] When automatic cars are sold on the open market, it will drastically change the dynamics of driving for everyone, and especially those who are unable to drive safely without assistance.

I imagine driverless cars will first become popular for older adults and adults with disabilities. I expect they will eventually be required for teenage drivers. (After adults over 70, teenagers are statistically the most dangerous drivers.) Once teens grow up with an automated driver, and automated cars are proven to reduce fatalities and accidents, our world will transition to automated vehicles. This chapter will be nearly obsolete! Until then, we have the following alternative approaches.

Family, Friends, and Neighbors

It's wonderful when neighbors can support each other. One key to success is having people who can make regular trips, such as grocery shopping, plus others who can help with irregular trips, such as gift shopping and doctor appointments.

At a glance:

- Sometimes neighbors can help
- Consider having one person for regular trips (such as grocery shopping) and another person for irregular trips (gift shopping, doctor appointments)
- It's very difficult to ask for help, so set up a system that minimizes the feeling your loved one is a burden to others.
- Consider a way to return the favor to helpers, which helps preserve dignity, such as paying for gas, treating them to a meal, etc.

Public Transportation

This is a good option that allows for a higher degree of independence. If your loved one can learn a new routine, public transportation may be a good option. If so, help your loved one learn the routes by traveling on common routes with them the first time. It will give you a chance to see if they are comfortable with the system. You can help find routes, times, and payment methods.

If Alzheimer's begins to set in, watch for the time when public transportation is no longer a viable option. Common markers are confusion, disorientation, and getting lost.

At a glance:

- Allows for a higher degree of independence
- Make sure they can learn a new routine

- Help your loved one learn the routes by traveling on common routes with them the first time
- Watch to make sure public transportation remains a viable option, especially for those with dementia.

Taxi Service/Uber
Taxis and Uber or Lyft also provide high independence without having to ask for help. They also make a great back-up if family or friends are unavailable to help. Of course, some regions provide better taxi service than others. Again, if your loved one has not taken a taxi or used an online driving service before, accompany them on the first couple trips, so they can learn the system of calling for a ride, communicating with a driver, and paying fare.

At a glance:

- Provides a high independence without having to ask for help
- A great back-up if family or friends are unavailable to help
- Some regions don't offer adequate taxi service
- If your loved one has not used this mode of transportation before, accompany them on the first couple trips, so they can learn the system.

Special Transportation Services
Some communities have special services for elder adults, including dedicated buses with door-to-door

services. The Eldercare Locator at www.eldercare. acl.gov provides information on region-specific resources.

Considerations:

- What is the cost? Do passengers tip drivers? Can you set up an account for payment?
- How often can the service be used? Is it only for medical visits and grocery shopping?
- Will drivers provide assistance for people with disabilities or limitations?
- Can caregivers/companions accompany the eligible rider?

Both the Eldercare Locator and the Alzheimer's Organization offer great articles and resources addressing the driving issue.

Public transportation doesn't work for everyone though. It's difficult to learn a new system at 88 years old. And it doesn't work in every situation. It may be fine for getting to a doctor appointment. It wouldn't work for weekly shopping trips when there are more bags than one or two people can carry. (Consider a trip to the grocery store. Are you usually able to walk out carrying all of your purchases? Or do you need a cart?)

Home deliveries are options for grocery shopping and some pharmacies. These types of services will greatly facilitate caregiving and help our loved ones maintain independence longer.

The end of driving means the start of significant interdependence, and the need for others to be regularly involved in an elder's life.

What's Next?
It's important to help our loved ones recognize and make the transition away from driving when it becomes a danger. When that day arrives, we need to help them find a way to continue functioning without being able to hop in the car at will. Reduced mobility sometimes means a new living situation is required. Navigation guides for that decision come next.

Chapter 4

Where Should Dad Live?

Love begins at home, and it is not how much we do, but how much love we put into that action.
—*Mother Teresa*

A house is not a home unless it contains food and fire for the mind as well as the body.
—*Benjamin Franklin*

Time for Change
When Grandma fell and broke her hip, she landed in a rehabilitation facility for a 30-day stay. Suddenly, without warning, everything changed. There wasn't much decision making involved.

Whether it happens suddenly or slowly over time, if your loved one lives long enough, they will likely need some kind of assistance to keep on living. That in turn results in a change to their living situation. How can we help our loved ones plan for the future, so they finish their days well?

My aunt Grace moved to be near her children and grandchildren after her husband passed on. In time, she moved to senior retirement housing. She lived there for 10 years. She played in Bridge clubs and made friends in her community. It was a great set-up until Grace's daughters discovered she didn't remember whether she had eaten dinner. When they observed more, they found she had either been skipping meals or eating two meals, because she couldn't remember whether she'd eaten. Nor did she recall if she'd taken her medications.

After a diagnosis of Alzheimer's disease and seeing a need for more care, her daughters offered Grace to move in with them or to move into an assisted living facility. She chose assisted living. What would your loved one chose, given an option?

Individualized Solutions

I am a proponent of individualized solutions. One size does not fit all. Should you move your parent into your home? The answer depends on your parent's ability and willingness to move—along with their level of ability to live independently, your ability to provide support, finances, and local resources. It's complex.

We can't be guaranteed the outcome will work the way we hope. Asking advice from others may help. Only time will reveal the outcome. The most important thing is to look, listen, care, and act when it's time to act. We can only do our best with what we have. Understanding the pros and cons helps the decision-making process.

This chapter will outline factors to consider in making a change. In addition to finding an affordable solution, consider the level of change required for each person involved, the level of independence that can be maintained for your loved one (reaching for the highest level), and the physical and emotional needs of each person involved.

Options

❏ **Move into your loved one's home**

❏ **Move loved one into your home**

❏ **Moving loved one to an assisted living center**

❏ **Hire a live-in caregiver or helper**

The Logistics of Moving into Their Home

Pros: Huge benefit emotionally and psychologically for person receiving care.

- Less change for your loved one. No packing. No new doctors. No address change.
- Your loved one can keep many of the same systems and patterns for daily living. This allows for greater independence, which aids in motivation for living.
- Loved one keeps the same social networks. This significantly helps maintain emotional well-being and motivation for living.
- In some cases, lower cost of living with combined financial resources. (If the loved one is your spouse, consider having a relative move in to help?)

Cons: This can be a huge sacrifice for the caregiver.

- Loved one must create space for you. Loved one must make adjustments to living.
- You must adjust and adapt your life to someone else's. You are not king or queen of the house. That may mean changes in eating and sleeping patterns.
- May bring conflict, since each person brings unique expectations and habits.
- You may experience the physical, emotional toll of a full-time caregiver.

Words of wisdom from those who have done it:

- This is a great way to preserve the dignity and in-dependence of your loved one.
- It can require significant personal sacrifices.

The Logistics of Moving Someone into Your Home

Pros: You can maintain much of your lifestyle, and have more control of many factors.

- You know the care your loved one is receiving.
- You get to be the primary source of blessing for your loved one's final years.
- This option may be better than a nursing home or hiring a live-in helper in your loved one's home. Of course, if you are caring for a married couple, it's important to keep them together. (If the loved one is your spouse, seek a caring expert for advice and support.)

Cons: Your loved one may not be happy with the move. It's a major change.

- Your loved one moves into a new home. This kind of major change can result in depression. If they move out of town or out of state, they lose their primary social support network, need to create new routines at home, live under someone else's roof and therefore "rules."
- You may experience the physical, emotional toll of a full-time carer.

Words of wisdom from those who have done it:

- You are the primary caregiver for your loved one. That's both a pro and a con.
- If your loved one has dementia, the move can be very disorienting. For example, they may have trouble knowing where to find things. In fact, they may never learn where the bathroom is, and therefore need help finding it each time. (This happened to a couple in our Alzheimer's class.)

The Logistics of Moving Someone to a Facility (such as Assisted Living Centers)

Pros: Sometimes our loved ones need more care than we can possibly give them.

- When our loved one doesn't want to burden us, yet needs a little or a lot of help with daily living, these facilities can help.

- If the facility offers progressive levels of assistance, it may make changes in care much easier, because your loved one won't have to move out of the area, and can maintain established relationships. For example, transferring from basic assisted living to dementia care.

- Workers at these care centers understand the ins and outs of helping elderly persons with daily living.

- There is potential for community and meaningful relationships with peers.

- In many cases, a professional nurse is on site.

Cons: Multiple major considerations are listed here.

- There can be a considerable financial cost. Some cost $3,000–5,000 per month, plus a start-up fee.

- Most times, our loved ones understand that this is a "final destination" of sorts. The fact that they are losing their home and independence is undeniable. That can lead to depression or lack of motivation to go on, particularly if they are resistant to the move.

- Potential for abusive situations. There are many good, caring helpers at facilities. There are also some burned-out and underpaid workers. However, it only takes one abusive person to make a situation unbearable. You must remain involved and keep an eye out for potential abuse.

- If you suspect abuse in a care facility, contact the ombudsman. The number for the local ombudsman must be posted in every facility. You can also call the Eldercare Locator service at 1-800-677-1116 to find the your area ombudsman.

- Don't be surprised if your loved one develops a significant, romantic relationship late in life with another resident. (While not necessarily a "con," their children often find it unsettling.)

Words of wisdom from those who have done it:

- As much as possible, visit and spend time with your loved one when they are in a care facility. This will help avoid potentially abusive situations. Your presence communicates to your loved one and everyone else who sees you visit that they are loved. Your loved one will likely receive better care when others see you visit.

- Check out this link on Long-Term Resident Care Dignity. Another helpful resource is nursinghome411.org/fact-sheet-standards-for-nursing-home-services.

Hiring a Live-In Caregiver or Helper Options

When a loved one only needs minimal assistance, such as someone to help with emergencies, or help with shopping or cooking, some families offer low rent in return for occasional help. In some cases a neighbor offers to help.

Another option is hiring a full-time or part-time care giver to assist with daily living. Usually, this occurs though an agency, which is recommended, so that there is a background check and accountability for the workers.

While each of these situations differ somewhat, the guiding principles for success, and some of the risks, remain the same.

Pros:

- This may provide a solution for your loved one to stay at home with as much independence as possible.

Cons:

- Not all helpers are adequately trained.
- Not all helpers are helpful.
- Risk for abuse, theft, and conflict.

Words of wisdom from those who have done it:

- Be aware of risks in this tricky situation. You must be aware of laws, such as laws regarding payment and liability insurance.

- You must be watchful to avoid scams, such as a caregiver gaining power of attorney over your loved one. Investigate the background of those invited to live with or regularly assist your loved one.
- Stop by the house unannounced to check on level of care. (Or install cameras in the house.)
- Watch closely to see when it's time to change from this limited level of care to more involved care.

More on Helper Scenario

Ironically, this less-recommended care scenario requires the most information.

Ideal situation for a live-in helper or neighbor helper:

- Your loved one needs help running errands when unable to drive.
- Your loved one needs occasional help with certain tasks, such as lifting something heavy.
- Your loved one needs help keeping the house clean.
- Your loved one wants someone available to help as needs arise.
- The live-in renter is a sort of companion, so your loved one is not all alone should they fall, start having accidents or other challenges.

In these ways, a renter both helps your loved one stay independent for as long as possible, and is able to alert you in case the need for help grows greater. In some cases, especially where a dementia does not develop, a live-in companion helper may be just what is needed.

Remember to take proper steps to ensure the safety of your loved one if you choose to have a renter-helper. There is more on this at the end of the chapter.

If your loved one needs regular help preparing meals, taking medications, bathing, and more, it's time to consider professional care or stepping in yourself. If your loved one develops a dementia, such as Alzheimer's, you can expect the day will come when the renter-helper (and neighbor-helper) does not provide the necessary level of support.

The family must prepare for that change, checking in regularly with both carer and loved one, and keeping an open line of communication for the carer to report changes or needs. The family must plan for the time when full-time care is needed.

Define Expectations for Helper

Provide absolutely clear communication about expectations (in other words, both verbally and in writing). Everyday office jobs use a job description defining the expectations of the employer and the scope of work. There is usually a supervisor to see that work is actually being completed, and to provide guidance in performing tasks. Likewise, there should be a clear list of duties expected for a live-in carer.

For example, the phrase "help with housework" is not clear enough. We all have different ideas of what that represents. Make the list comprehensive, including all desired services: vacuum house, clean bathroom, clean kitchen, take mom to the store weekly for groceries, take mom to run errands. Make the list as specific as the things you wish to see done.

"Companion" also needs to be defined. It helps to establish the number of hours per week or day the live-in carer is expected to help, interact, and be present. It also defines what is meant by companionship, whatever it may be, such as taking a walk or watching TV.

Karen's Case

Karen offers one example of a neighbor-carer arrangement. This arrangement worked well in the beginning, but as Karen's needs grew greater, there came a time when a neighbor-helper was no longer the answer.

Karen is an elderly woman whose family lives out of state. Since Karen's neighbor Abigail was willing to help, the family hired Abigail to look after her.

After a year with this agreement, Karen, who lives alone, became concerned that someone was breaking into her house at night, stealing food and leaving a mess. She was very upset about this situation and found it happening frequently.

There is one problem: The break-ins are all her imagination. No amount of reasoning helps and Karen feels insecure at home.

The presumed break-ins happen every time unclean dishes are left in the sink overnight. Abigail goes to Karen's home every 2-3 days to clean the dishes, but not every night. (Changing that one factor could significantly keep Karen from living in fear and worry all day.)

Abigail is an untrained, nonprofessional helper. She doesn't visit Karen every day. Karen's need for help has extended beyond what Abigail is willing and able to provide, even though Abigail is paid.

It's time for Karen's family to step in. Being far away, it is difficult for them to realize just how much their help is needed and that it's needed right away. Not only is Karen living in fear, she is displaying symptoms of dementia. She may also have trouble taking her medications and eating regularly. If she has a fall or serious illness, it could take a day or two before she gets help.

Karen's story illustrates the need for clearly defined help, as well as continued family involvement, and responding to changes as life goes on.

Fortunately, Abigail was a kind and helpful neighbor. What if the helper hired does not turn out to be so selfless? What other considerations should a family make before hiring someone to go into the home?

Necessary Arrangements for Hired Helper

Renting a room to someone in exchange for care-giving support services can work, yet it's very risky, and requires much more planning than the average family is prepared for. You are asking a stranger to live with and care for your loved one.

The pesky, necessary steps to take when someone pays partial rent for services:

- Get a full background check.
- Legitimate references: Due diligence can save headaches. While anyone can provide fake references, it may be possible to find some legitimate ones.
- Liability insurance: in case the helper falls or gets hurt.
- Power of attorney: so that the helper doesn't take that function for you.
- Written agreement: so there is a contract regarding the agreement of exchange. This is needed in case a helper sues for pay or decides not to help.
- Store and document valuables: Move those valuables that can be stored or locked up. Make documentation of other valuables. Consider how finances are handled. Is there a checkbook in the house? Credit cards? How can you monitor those to prevent theft?

Decision

Which scenario best fits you and your loved one? Sometimes circumstances naturally limit the options. It's up to us to make the best of the situation. Knowing some of the pros, cons, and potential pitfalls will help you prepare for the transition. It's one of the biggest decisions you will make in caregiving. After that, you'll begin wading in deeper waters of caregiving. The next several chapters discuss how to do that well, beginning with making difficult decisions in everyday life.

Chapter 5

Difficult Decisions

"I found my 80-year-old mother with Alzheimer's outside cutting down a tree with a chainsaw. I wasn't sure whether or not to stop her while the chainsaw was still running."
— member of an anonymous support group

Chest Pains and Little Imps

It's my responsibility to call 911, an unspoken but understood designation. I feel fairly comfortable with making that decision. I've only had to do it twice, and both times were well-justified. Such as the time Grandma had heart-attack symptoms. From her obvious pain and the tears running down her face, I knew we didn't have time to negotiate, only time to call for help.

There are half-a-dozen other times that I considered calling but didn't. Fortunately, those decisions ultimately proved okay, though at the time I couldn't be sure. Like the times in the middle of the night Grandpa woke up with chest pains and wanted me to drive him to the hospital. Even as I write, I think, "Why didn't I call 911?!"

It would've made perfect sense to call. Only I was still new in my role and Grandpa vehemently opposed going to the ER in an ambulance.

It is exactly those times that taught me how to make difficult decisions for my family members. The real difficulty lies in the complex social roles and norms of the family, and the need to turn them upside down in certain situations. After all, my grandparents are in charge of their own lives and home. For my 40 years on earth, they have been the ones to help rear me and give me advice on life. Sometimes I think they still see a lanky, unpredictable twelve-year-old when they look at me.

How then can I overrule their expressed decisions or desires—sometimes breathed with unflexing vehemence? I, the younger, less-experienced imp who lives with them? (I am guessing that's what they feel at times.)

As a sensitive person, I consider their point-of-view. How awful to have someone come in and tell you what to do with your life, when you already know quite well what you want!

When it's time to "parent your parents" life feels upside down to everyone involved. I'm sure it's quite the same for non-family caregivers, hired to help and even supervise another person. It's extremely complex!

That complexity, with or without adding the attempt to preserve respect and dignity, brings about the need to make difficult decisions. And, as we well know, making no decision *is* a decision. No decision on whether to call 911 results in a decision not to call 911. The bottom line (and my personal guiding factor) is that the safety, health, and well-being of the other person is the first priority.

Where money is no issue, the decision to call 911 should be easy. In the lives of ordinary people, we can easily say, "Better to call than not to call; better to be safe than sorry." In the complex world of elder care, where Grandpa has chest pains four times in one month (none of which turned out to be a heart attack), and lives on a limited fixed income, does it make sense to call 911 at every turn? Add that he's begging me not to call.

In the fiery moments it's sometimes hard to know what to do. Two factors help me decide: the choice that safety and health overrules doubts, and advance preparation for potential emergencies.

Advance Plan

It helps to think through situations in advance—know your options. What are the symptoms of a heart attack and stroke? When do those symptoms warrant immediate medical attention? Sometimes an upset, gassy stomach mimics heart attack symptoms. Is there a way to know the difference between indigestion and a life-threatening moment?

When Grandma's speech became slurred, mimicking a possible stroke, I jumped to action: made sure she was sitting and stayed seated (she wanted to walk around), had her lift both arms in the air (to see if one side of the body couldn't respond), stick out her tongue, and repeat a sentence back to me. I also stayed calm, spoke calmly, and did all of the actions I asked her to do. I raised my arms, stuck out my tongue, etc. Ask your doctor what to do if you suspect a stroke. Most protocols say go straight to the hospital, because every minute of treatment from the start of the stroke can make a difference in recovery for strokes.

I cannot emphasize enough the value of being prepared for real health emergencies.

Where is the nearest or best emergency center? You must know. You also *must* know if your loved one has a DNR (a do not resuscitate form), and you must know where it is. You need to have insurance information. You need to know health conditions (diabetes, heart disease), what medications they take, who their primary physician is, when is the last time they had surgery (requiring anesthetic), and allergies (allergic to penicillin or latex, etc.).

Did I just overwhelm you? That's not nearly as overwhelmed as you'll feel if you face a real emergency without vital information. You need to know this for yourself also, and you need someone else to know it for you. It's one of those things you can't afford to put off.

Check out logistics in chapter 10. It goes over the forms and information you need to have ready before the emergency.

Non-Emergencies

Not all difficult decisions involve life-or-death scenarios. Most of them are everyday decisions. For example, should we put a handle bar in the shower stall for Grandpa?

Grandpa has been resisting the handle bar for the last few years, while Grandma has been pushing it. He has been successful until now. Now things are changing. Unfortunately, his legs are weakening and he has to use a cane to get around. However, Grandpa is afraid that a handle bar will devalue the house and that a water pipe may be hit during installation.

He won the no-handle-bar battle until the week he fell twice in the shower. On the side of compassion, my heart goes out to him. How awful to fall in the shower at all, not to mention twice in one week! Plus, his family knows about it, which is embarrassing. And now he's afraid to take a shower. Nonetheless, he doesn't want a handle bar in his shower. His world is changing in ways he never wanted. It stinks.

Sometimes we have to do things we don't want to do, the greater good among two evils. We have to place short- and long-term health and safety above our comforts and above sometimes distorted judgment.

Stepping In, Backing Off

I have learned through fiery experiences that it's better to step in and assert myself when safety is an issue. My decision overrides theirs when they don't make a balanced decision with regard to a safety matter. Even when they are angry with me, I must make the responsible decision. "Sit down in this chair. I'm going to call 911."

Not all decisions are clear cut. It's not always obvious when to draw the line. That's part of the difficulty—for both me and them. If I consistently step in too soon, trying to assert authority unnecessarily, I may be causing more harm than good. I may be hindering their happiness instead of enhancing their latter years. More often than not, I suspect, my decisions are a mixture of help and hindrance. It is like a dance to be learned. There are so many missteps initially, but as I keep working at it, I minimize mistakes and it can become a beautiful thing.

The point is to avoid a rigid, over-bearing approach. Half the time, when I refrain from insisting doing something my way (what seems the best solution to me) it turns out fine without me in the mix.

I learned that lesson from hanging clothes outside. For a while, I thought I should hang the clothes on the line, rather than Grandma, for her safety. I hated hanging the clothes instead of using the drier, but that was beside the point. Grandma had broken her hip when she fell on the uneven lawn a few years before, and she was concerned about her shoulder with a rotator cuff tear. That I should start hanging the laundry for her seemed obvious to me.

She resisted the idea, so it became a race—who would get outside first to hang the clothes when the washer stopped? When I got out first, she'd still come out and we'd hang laundry side-by-side. That wasn't such a bad thing. Only I didn't hang clothes her way, which bugged her so much that she would sometimes re-do my work. That in turn frustrated me. It was a lose-lose situation.

After a while, I discovered that Grandma can hang laundry just fine without me. So I backed off. Despite her shoulder pain, it is a good way for her to exercise her arms regularly. She hasn't fallen again (that I'm aware of). When she wants help hanging clothes, she lets me know. If clothes are still on the line after dark, or on a day when she's unsteady, I go take care of it. That discovery and adjustment eliminated a source of frustration from my day and hers.

Grandma even admitted recently that someday she won't be able to do the laundry. Until then, it's all hers!

Figuring It Out

There is no fast-and-set rule for making difficult decisions for those we care for. Developing guidelines for your scenario can help you when you face those moments. I hope the examples given help as you navigate difficult decisions.

There's also the wonderful psychological tool called "detachment" that helps us see our path more clearly. It means stepping back and looking at the situation as an outsider, so I can consider the situation without emotional attachments. In other words, if I came across a stranger who was having these symptoms, what would I do? That detachment helps me separate emotions from fact when Grandpa says he doesn't want to see a doctor.

Another great tool for making difficult decisions, especially if the decision is not required immediately, is talking with others. Others can provide insight and input, plus help share the burden, relieving stress. They can also be a source of confirmation and encouragement.

Split-Second Grace

Advanced preparation for difficult decisions has helped me make good choices in critical decision moments. It's helped me dial 911 at the right time, instead of waiting too long.

A word about split-second decisions: I give myself a lot of grace for those moments. Right or wrong, I do my best. I also pray and expect God to help and guide me. God hasn't let me down.

If my decision, action, or choice wasn't perfect, I don't beat myself up. If all turns out well, I breathe a sigh of relief. Give yourself grace to make mistakes and be less than perfect, knowing that your presence makes a difference for the better.

While this chapter encourages stepping in, especially when safety is at stake, the next chapter insists on keeping out where we're not really needed.

Chapter 6

Maintaining Independence

"Are you aiming to sustain independence?"
asked the visiting nurse.

TLQ

Total life quality. That is our goal. Finishing well, as well as possible, given all the circumstances and variables, is our aim. The circumstances change continually and unpredictably, requiring us to adjust also. The formula for maintaining quality of life can't be served in a single cup.

The intangibles, those things that exist though we can't touch them with our fingers, are some of the most important ingredients for success. Love is the most obvious. Dignity is also right up at the top. And one we won't recognize it until we begin to lose it: independence.

Independence and dignity go hand-in-hand.

This is the great challenge, because as we lose our ability to do what we've always done, we begin to lose our independence. Dignity, also invisible to the eye but felt in the soul, takes a hit.

Helping Out

When I first recognized my role as a caregiver with my grandparents, I thought I was here to help. I was wrong, wrong, wrong.

Have you ever tried to help someone who didn't want help? It doesn't usually turn out well. It's a rather presumptuous thing to do. Just because someone might benefit from help doesn't mean they want it or need it.

How can we remove presumption from the equation? *Simply ask if help is wanted.* That allows fellow humans to maintain independence.

For example, Grandpa and Grandma's large yard needed to be watered twice a week. I viewed it as a somewhat laborious task, hauling out the long, heavy hose and going all around the yard. So on watering day I'd dash outside and do it before Gram. Then I found out that Gram loves being in the yard. She doesn't view watering as a chore. So I needed to step back. Instead, I'd ask if she wanted me to water that day.

When Grandma decided to can the pears from her yard, I decided to help. Instead, I got in the way. I didn't cut the pears by her standards. She had a system for the whole process and I didn't know it. She was frustrated; I was frustrated. I gave up and left the kitchen.

"I'm just trying to help!" played in my head.

Then I realized that the real goal wasn't to help with all of life. My real purpose for living with Grandpa and Grandma is to help them live at home, as long as possible, with the best quality of life. My goal, specifically, is to help them maintain independence.

There is a subtle yet clear difference between the two approaches. It is all in my attitude. And that attitude is revealed in my actions. When I keep in mind the proper goal of maintaining independence, I am a great help. When I slip back into the idea that I'm "here to help" I step on their toes and inadvertently work against the real goal.

Your Way or My Way?

One of the ways the help-versus-independence approach plays out is whether I insist on doing something my way or do it their way. The difference seemed so subtle on the surface, I didn't initially recognize that I was really interfering instead of helping when I stepped in with the wrong approach.

It takes time to learn someone else's method of performing tasks. After living with them for a couple of years, I learned Gram wasn't happy with the way I watered the yard, which is part of the reason she resisted letting me do it. She wanted each plant watered for exactly 20 seconds, with 30 seconds for the Bird of Paradise plant. She literally counted seconds for each plant.

Once I understood the difference and importance of handling their affairs their way, it made life easier for them. When Grandpa decided to have me help handle the bills, I continued to use his system of mailing in checks. I didn't switch to my preferred system of paying online. He signed all of the checks after I wrote them out and it kept him in control.

Doing it someone else's way takes humility (not counting my way as the right way or the best way) and selflessness (because it makes me servant, not master of the task). Maybe that's why it was so hard for me in the beginning. For those humble, gentle, don't-need-to-be-in-charge souls caring for a relative, this may already come naturally.

Driving is a big part of independence. What about life after driving? Can Grandma decide when to go shopping, or does it depend on my schedule? Now that we have an interdependent relationship, we work together in each other's reality. I may not be able to take her shopping at her preferred time due to a pre-existing appointment, but I can take her to her preferred store. Since I am the chauffeur and she is in charge, it all runs smoothly. If I were to attempt to insert my agenda or insist on a different store, it would be a mess.

Use It or Lose It
The axiom proves true for much of life. The longer life goes on, the more things our elders give up doing because they can't. However, we must encourage our loved ones to continue doing as much as they can as long as they can. Usually, they already have the drive and desire to keep taking care of themselves. Even if a task takes longer, even when it's harder, help your loved one keep doing things for themselves as much as possible. Once we take over a function or chore and do it for them, they will soon lose the ability to do it. It will fall out of their repertoire.

It may seem silly, but going shopping, washing clothes or dishes, putting a pill box together, and other chores gives a person something to do each day. It's a necessary part of life.

When Grandpa couldn't button his shirt anymore because the small buttons were difficult to handle, he used a special device to button his own shirt. It took 20 minutes sometimes, but he did it himself.

My first impulse when I saw him struggling that much to button his shirt was to step in and help. However, that would've been a failure on my part! It's better not to take away the things he can still do. Sometimes helping is as easy as staying out of the way. That is what it means to promote independence instead of "helping."

Creative Problem Solving

When we work toward independence for our loved ones, we will sometimes hit a genuine road block. Logistical, practical, and safety issues arise as memory, coordination, or judgment diminish. For example, at our house utility bills were being lost and going unpaid, resulting in termination of service, plus late fees. When it happened repeatedly, I had to find a way to change things. I wanted to pull all of the bills out of the mail delivery, so they wouldn't get lost. Yet pulling all the bills out of the mail would take away Grandpa's job of sorting mail.

I needed a different way to succeed. It called for creative thinking. In the end, all I had to do was make a list of their monthly and annual bills, and check them off the list as they got paid. If I got to the end of the month and a bill wasn't checked off, I knew about it before it became a problem. The problem was solved with Grandpa's job still intact.

You get the picture. Changes continue to occur over time, requiring multiple adjustments over time. What works today may not work next month. So build in the practice using creative approaches to sustain independence at the start. Ask, "Is there another way to do this?"

Partner-Participant

If your loved one has a dementia, like Alzheimer's, as time goes on those kinds of daily tasks will become more difficult for your loved one to do independently. In that case there is a choice: to do the chore for them or be a partner-participant. Enabling someone else to continue the task takes more time and patience. It can be a full-time job requiring 100% attention. Yet, it's a worthwhile investment.

When Grandma puts her pills together (instead of me doing it for her) she is living for herself. Over time, she began making a lot of mistakes, sometimes doubling, sometimes skipping medications. So I sit with her and watch her put the pills in the box. It'd be far easier and faster for me to do it. Yet if I did, it'd be one less thing for her to do. If she had no daily tasks, what would she do? Watch TV all day? She wouldn't like that.

Research Says

Making patients with Alzheimer's too dependent on their caregivers may make them less likely to contribute to daily activities and, in the process, diminish their sense of self-worth.

"Often caregivers are only trying to help by assuming many of the day-to-day tasks that the person with Alzheimer's needs. But when the caregiver assumes too many duties, it can create a so-called 'dependency support script,'" Ms. Rust says, in which those with Alzheimer's are not encouraged to do things for themselves. As a result, the person with Alzheimer's may feel less inclined to get involved with tasks like helping out in the kitchen or getting dressed that they may well be capable of, particularly in the earlier stages of the disease.[5]

Having something to do provides purpose and meaning in life. As much as we'd all like to take an extended vacation in life, the truth is, we will become depressed if we don't have something meaningful to do. Our loved one will become depressed, discouraged, or despondent if there is nothing to do and no reason to keep doing it.

If Dementia Steps In

If your loved one is losing the ability to complete tasks independently due to an advancing disease, building routines and establishing patterns helps set the stage for maintaining independence in completing tasks. (This holds true for most of us.) If we establish that Tuesday after lunch is the time to put the pills together, and we have the pills in a certain place, with a place and pattern for putting them together, it goes more smoothly than completing the task at a random place or time.

When it's detected early, many adults who know about their own diagnosis of Alzheimer's plan and prepare for the stages and changes to come. I have seen families in this situation in advance-planning mode. It's powerful to communicate personal desires and plans in advance. I applaud them for their courage and determined efforts.

Whether or not we know in the early stages of such a disease, there is help from all around. Reach out and get that help! It will keep you from sinking. It will help you finish well.

What If Your Loved One Is in a Care Facility?

In short-term rehabilitative care, the nurses and staff will work hard at helping your loved one maintain independence.

If your loved one is in a permanent care facility, you will have to help them build and maintain as much independence as possible. Can he get into the wheelchair and move around the hall? Can she go join in the activities? Help your loved one stay active and involved. Don't do for them what they can do for themselves. Use creative problem solving to maintain points of independence. Encourage them to keep on going by building quality of life that comes from taking care of ourselves and having something meaningful to do.

Highlights for Success

Maintaining independence is a crucial component in safeguarding quality of life. What can we do to maintain independence?

- Keep the real goal in mind: helping our loved one maintain as much independence as possible.
- Ask first before helping.
- Consider not offering to help if our loved one can complete the task independently.
- Be an assistant or partner-participant with a task rather than taking over the job.

This chapter may seem counter-intuitive. After all, this book advocates that we step in to help, right? That's right. And now we're talking about how to do it well. This is the part you don't find in many caregiving books. It means there is a wrong way to help. I know because that's how I started—right motives, wrong methods. The next few chapters describe other intangibles that every caregiver needs to know. It's the difference between "making it through" versus finishing well.

Chapter 7

Dignity

It is very possible that you will find human beings,
surely very near you, needing affection and love.
Do not deny them these. Show them, above all,
that you sincerely recognize that they are human
beings, that they are important to you.
—*Mother Teresa,* In My Own Words

Personhood

Dignity is tied to personhood. It means we are human, not animal, not object. It means choice, volition, rights. It deems respect. Oftentimes, we tie it to ability, such as ability to perform tasks. Therefore, when a person is unable to perform an everyday action on their own, and becomes dependent on another to aid, dignity is threatened.

Along with maintaining independence and promoting quality of life, dignity is one of the intangibles we caregivers give special attention to, so that our aging loved one finishes well. Living with dignity, versus without, is crucial for true quality of life. Without it, we are reduced to inhuman life, like an animal or inanimate object.

Dignity is notoriously difficult to define. Yet we are hyper-aware when our dignity is demeaned or endangered. We find dignity in ourselves, and we receive it from others. It mimics self-respect in that way. To elaborate, it is possible for me to keep my self-respect, even if someone loses respect for me. And it's possible for me to not respect myself, even when others respect me. Therefore, we must always view the person in our care with dignity and respect.

Dignity is threatened as dependency on others increases. This is the everyday challenge of our aging loved one. First, they must depend on someone else to do the driving. Usually that means asking for help. In fact, now they must ask for help with more and more things, from making a phone call to making dinner to just simply watching the TV (thanks to complex remote controls or unfamiliar technology). As time goes on, that aid may extend to daily personal care, such as bathing and toilet trips.

Therefore, at the very beginning of physical or mental decline, we must keep the bar of dignity held high. Just as we can encourage self-respect in someone who has lost it, so can we instill the sense of dignity in another. As we join our loved one in this most challenging walk, we have the privilege of making it dignified.

The following anecdotes address some common dignity-threatening scenarios we face on the journey.

No Scolding

One of the awful parts of growing significantly older and increasingly dependent is that, not only do our own bodies begin to act in undignified ways, other people around us do too.

I was guilty of this offense. When Grandpa had to begin using a walker, he resisted strongly. Press pause for a moment. I know that I will not be happy the day I need to use a walker. And if people force me to use it when I don't think I need it? Even worse! I felt compassion for him. However, safety trumped personal preference. He had fallen five times in the span of one month. Thank God he hadn't broken a bone.

I thought the compassion I felt covered the offense of forcing him to use the walker. As with anyone learning a new habit, or forced to do something they don't want to do, he frequently left his walker behind instead of using it. In my mind, he was walking away whenever he could get away with it. My perception of his motives was not positive, not giving him the benefit of the doubt.

"Grandpa, don't forget your walker," I would say as I saw him walking away from it. This happened various times and various ways, with various tones of voice.

Again, he had to learn to use it as a habit. He also needed motivation, which was mainly provided via insistence or nagging from others. Grandma had well-established the nagging pattern through the years, which I hated, yet acknowledged was sometimes the only way to get results.

One day I saw someone else get on his case about using the walker. I didn't like the way it looked or sounded. It seemed like they were shaking a finger at him, scolding this honorable war veteran in his own home. It just wasn't right.

Tone of voice plays a big role in communicating attitudes, such as respect or scolding.

From that time on I stopped saying, "Where's your walker?" or "You're forgetting something!" Instead, I'd go find the walker and bring it to him. That action presumes innocence (for example, that he forgot about it). It does not scold, nor does it suggest purposeful negligence. In fact, it merely suggests that I noticed something out of place and provided a remedy.

When I bring it to him, he usually says something like, "It walked away from me!" And we both laugh. It's much more dignified.

Isn't this supposed to be the age of respect? Yet so often it turns out the opposite.

On a Need to Know Basis

I will always remember when it got to the point where I couldn't leave either of them alone at home. They'd had several significant mishaps when I was out. (This happened as Alzheimer's began to progress for both of them.) It was at that point I told my dad and uncle that I needed another person at the house to handle caregiving.

When I was home alone with them on the week-days, I couldn't take Grandma grocery shopping without leaving Grandpa alone at home. Shopping with Grandma was a three-hour tour. I didn't have a neighbor or friend who could spare that much time on a weekday afternoon.

I feared that if I told her, "I don't want to leave Grandpa home alone," she would repeat it to him loud and clear. That would be pretty awful and offend his sense of dignity!

At the same time I was in a quagmire, because I couldn't just say no when she wanted to go shopping. So I said a prayer, took a deep breath, and privately told her. She agreed that she also didn't want him to be alone. She also agreed that telling him wouldn't be good. In that way, I got her buy in on the idea that we shouldn't tell him. Getting her buy-in, so that she was also responsible for the decision, made it work well. And knowing Grandma, I reminded her not to tell him.

In this way we managed to protect Grandpa's dignity, while also making sure that our logistics worked. I could take her shopping as long as someone else was home to be with Grandpa. In an ironic twist the "not home alone" umbrella also applied to her.

Not Children

What other situations in life do we not leave someone home alone? We find it most commonly with children. Children have dignity to be respected. It stands in effect apart from the fact that they are dependent on and under the authority of parents or guardians. They are small people who claim 100% personhood, with their own feelings, preferences, and wills.

Because a caregiving situation is sometimes similar to a parent-child relationship, the same kind of relational-dynamic can naturally occur. Any adult would be offended if they were treated like a child by others. (For example, having something explained, as if they aren't smart enough to understand or know something.) Understanding and recognizing that dynamic helps us to avoid treating our loved ones that way.

As Grandma watches Grandpa lose his ability to comprehend complex matters, and sees him lose co-ordination so that he drops things while he eats, she begins to treat him like a child. She speaks to him in the tone of voice she uses with a small child. She overstates the obvious, "Here is the apple sauce." He grunts in dismay and says, "Yes, I can see that it's apple sauce!"

No matter how much people like to talk about a second childhood as we age, we are not children again. Be careful not to treat grown adults that way.

Bowels

These days Grandpa is reticent to leave the house. It makes me sad that he doesn't like to go out as much as he used to, but I understand the reason. As Alzheimer's progresses it becomes more difficult to handle the outside world, with myriad noisy sounds and visual input. However, it's the fear of losing his bowels in public that really keeps Grandpa from going out.

Even at home, he often races to the bathroom to avoid spillage. Occasionally, he doesn't make it to the toilet on time. It's dreadful to him, as it would be for anyone in that situation. We have seen doctors and tried medications to help control the issue. It's helped somewhat. Yet former mishaps remain fixed in his mind, so the fear remains.

Ever tried talking with your parents about using an adult diaper? Even though I just wrote "daiper," I'd never say it. We don't have to think of it that way, although some people do. It can feel pretty lousy to have to use one. Yet I see them as life-savers. They enable us the freedom to go out in public (or even be at home) without the fear of colossal embarrassment.

So I when I decided to talk with Grandpa about it, I knew that my attitude and approach needed to preserve his dignity. I needed to highlight the positives and minimize the feeling that wearing adult incontinence protection was the equivalent of a diaper.

Here's what I didn't say: "Grandpa, it's time for you to start wearing Depends." "Grandpa, if you want to avoid accidents, you'd better use the adult diaper." "We are taking you out to dinner for your birthday, so you'll have to wear Depends."

Here's what I did: I had a conversation with him. (We've talked about bathrooms more than once, because it has come up multiple times.) I talk with him about going out somewhere, for example, to a memorial service for his friend. He tells me he wants to go, but he's afraid there won't be a bathroom nearby.

He tells me upfront that he is afraid he won't make it to the bathroom in time. I respond, "I hear you. That wouldn't be good." Then I say, "I know you really want to go to the memorial service. Have you considered using Depends? I know you're not used to those things, but they really help."

Really, the main difference in those approaches is simple: instead of telling him what to do, as if I'm in charge, I am reminding him of his options so that he can make a personal decision. (He knows who he is and what he wants. He knows who I am, and that a long time ago he changed my diapers.)

Another aspect is that I'm not uncomfortable with the subject. There could easily be discomfort or awkwardness. I learned to approach it without emotion, like a nurse changing a bedpan. It's just a fact of life. It's not a fun fact, but neither does it need to be treated like an awful thing.

I have learned to talk about all aspects of bodily function. I am not afraid of the word diarrhea. I know that if someone is constipated, natural products such as coffee and chocolate will help move things along. When I talk about a sensitive subject with objectivity and ease, my grandparents respond with ease and naturalness. It's so much nicer than awkward.

How Important Is It?

I have had to learn to let go of things that feel important to me, so that my grandparents can live with relative ease and dignity. One of those places is at the dinner table. Grandpa's hands shake, his muscles are less coordinated, and since one eye is blind, his depth perception is poor. Those things lead quickly to dropped food, stained shirts, and spilled drinks.

It turns out that it's more dignified to ignore a spill on his shirt, most times, than to try to point it out or help clean it up. He and Grandma often can't or don't see food dropped on the table or the floor. I have learned to wait until dinner is over to clean up those messes, even though everything inside me wants to clean it immediately.

Grandpa now pours way to much salad dressing on his lettuce. It looks more like a swimming pool than a salad bowl. It totally nags at me inside. But I ask myself, *how important is it?* It takes a lot of self-control to keep from saying something or putting it on his salad for him.

Sometimes when he pours the apple sauce in his bowl, his depth perception causes him to miss. When I see him pouring it close to the edge, something inside me reacts and I want desperately to pour it for him. But it's important to him to do it himself, so I must let go. I must control my emotions and find balance for when to step in and when to stay out.

It hurts his sense of dignity to have me step in. So I arrange the dinner table for optimum effectiveness for him. Then I have to let go of my emotions. His dignity is more important than my need for clean.

There have been, and will be, times when his dignity is compromised. My goal is to minimize those times. The dinner table is, so far, one place where I can set aside my goals for his sense of well-being.

Set the Standard

Once, when a distant relative visited, they asked about Grandpa right in front of him, as if he wasn't there. "How's his memory these days?" they asked me. "His memory is great!" I replied. Then I left the room, so that the person could not continue the conversation.

I draw a hard line when it comes to talking in front of Grandpa and Grandma as if they are not in the room. That's just disrespectful. Even if we are in the hospital, and they appear to be sleeping, I avoid such conversations. How do I know if they can or can't hear? By maintaining integrity and respect, I minimize the risk of disrespect.

When others, who may be less aware or less sensitive, find that I won't act that way, they learn not to act that way also.

As the primary caregiver, I set the standard for the attitude that we keep in the home.

On Another Note

When relatives ask about Grandpa and Grandma's condition, I'm happy to keep them up-to-date. I'm glad they care enough to ask. We have a private conversation where I can share appropriate details. "Grandpa has trouble understanding when people talk quickly. So he really appreciates it when people slow down to talk with him." That was a respectful and appropriate way to communicate with family and preserve his dignity.

In a Care Facility or Assisted-Living Home

Dignity, privacy, and personal preference face potential demise in care facilities and assisted-living homes. For some great insights and practical suggestions on preserving dignity in these living situations, check out online links from the Florida Health Care Association and the Long Term Care Community Coalition.[6]

Doctor Visits

Going to the doctor could be a chapter on its own. Sometimes just getting to a doctor's appointment requires overriding personal preference not to see a doctor, because genuine safety and well-being outweigh that preference.

What about interactions *in* the doctor's office?

When I first went into the examining room during a doctor visit, I was primarily there to listen and to take notes. Then I found that on occasion, Grandma or Grandpa would not accurately report the situation or condition. Sometimes they would forget to report a vital fact, or due to forgetfulness, not give an accurate report on symptom frequency or duration of a condition. For example, Grandma reported that she had pain in her hip for a week, when it had been a month.

I had to train myself how to behave in the doctor's office. I learned to report important points, and stay out of the ones that really didn't matter. I learned not to over correct things Grandma reported, such as when she would tell the doctors, "I stay on a diabetic diet." Twenty years ago she did. Now she doesn't. However, she still mentions it with pride. If it doesn't pertain to the problem at hand, I don't need to correct it.

I also push myself to get involved and ask questions that matter, such as, "What kind of side effects are common with that medication? What are the risks with that procedure? What treatment options are available?"

Over time, doctors began to recognize that Grandpa and Grandma needed someone who could hear and record what was said, and someone who could comprehend the diagnosis and implement care at home. They began speaking directly to me with their assessment.

It is a very natural dynamic to speak to the person who can hear and comprehend. Yet, as much as it was natural for me too, I felt uncomfortable with the situation. We were talking about a person who was right there in the room with us! How did Grandpa and Grandma feel when the doctor talked with me instead of them? It almost felt like a parent-child situation, with my grandparents as the child. Their dignity was threatened.

I found a couple tricks to resolve the problem indirectly, without even mentioning it. I found that if I kept my eyes on my grandparents, instead of keeping eye contact with the doctor, he would eventually shift his eyes back to them and speak to them directly. This happens every time like magic! After a while, it worked so that we all have the normal eye contact, with the main focus on communicating with Grandpa and Grandma.

Sometimes I would also redirect the conversation to Grandpa and Grandma by saying something like, "Are you getting this Grandma?" Or turn to Grandpa and say, "You've taken that antibiotic before, right?" Then I'd keep my eyes on my grandparent and the conversation would naturally shift back to them.

The Payoff

Preserving their dignity in this way is a win-win situation. It helps me be a better person. In the end, when all is said and done, when Grandpa and Grandma are no longer with us, I want to be able to look at our time together and feel good about the way I treated them. In the thick of the moment, it's often difficult to see what I'm doing and how I'm doing it. It's easier to do things my way, and to respond with my emotions, rather than put them first.

Why do we water the lawn at 11 p.m.? (When it's dark outside and I'm ready to be done with chores.) Because that's when Grandma wants to do it. She really doesn't want it watered at 5 p.m. Little things like that may seem crazy and inconvenient, but they don't stop the world from going around.

Someday, when I look back, I want to know that I did right by them, in the big things and the little things. And someday, when I find myself in their shoes, I want someone to do right for me. There is no guarantee I will be treated with dignity, and my doing that for Grandpa and Grandma doesn't mean that I deserve it more than anyone else. It just gives me hope that it's possible. And I can look back on our time together with a smile instead of regrets. They can live with me today, and I can live with myself later.

If you find that you have missed the mark in preserving dignity, don't get discouraged. We've all made mistakes. As you begin to operate with greater awareness and respect for dignity, your loved ones and people around you will notice. You have the knowledge and power to bring dignity to the remainder of days you have together. You get to make the difference.

Chapter 8

Quality of Life

There is no quote for this chapter. Only the smile on the face of our loved one when they are enjoying life at the moment.

Beyond Just Making It

At the end of a long day, I realize that except for breakfast and dinner, Grandpa has sat in his chair all day watching TV. No wonder he doesn't seem as cheerful as usual these days.

I can cook meals, clean the house, pick up prescriptions, and take Grandma to doctor appointments. Those are important, life-giving activities. But if it means that Grandpa is sitting in the same chair all day, doing nothing, I'm not satisfied with that. I'd rather spend some quality time with Grandpa, even if it means skipping laundry.

I'm not here only to help my grandparents live. I want them to live well. I want them, as much as possible, to enjoy life. For my grandparents, a big part of that is continuing to live in their own home, rather than an assisted-living facility. It takes a huge commitment just to make that possible. Yet, there is more to it than physically residing in the house.

Disappearing Act

Due to the progression of Alzheimer's disease, Grandpa's role in active life is ebbing away. He no longer does the driving. He is no longer responsible to pay the bills and manage the bank account. He doesn't do the yard work or heavy lifting around the house. He doesn't participate in his service club anymore, the Fleet Reserve Association (for Navy, Marines, and Coast Guard service members and retirees), so he doesn't need to send and receive email often. He can barely button his shirt each morning.

This check-out from active life can happen slowly over time, often the case with Alzheimer's disease, or in a suddenly moment, such as extended hospitalization. It highlights the need to focus on independent living as long as possible. Taking care of ourselves, and others, provides a powerful purpose and incentive in life—more than we realize before we lose the responsibility.

As Grandpa's role in life scales back considerably, there is a risk that he will feel less purpose in living. He already feels less able to do things. His dignity is at risk all the time, just from the threat of not making it to the bathroom in time.

Important Questions

So I ask myself, "Is there anything I can do to make today better for him? Can I do something to make his day enjoyable? To give him a way to interact and laugh or smile? To know he is loved and valued?"

The fewer responsibilities he has for independent living, the more important this question becomes, and the more difficult to find answers. So I think about what he likes to do most. What makes him happy?

Is there anything I can do to make today better for him?

Grand Examples

There are three things that really make Grandpa happy: getting the mail, drinking a milk shake, and telling stories. He really feels good when doing those things. So I make sure he gets exactly that.

Grandpa missed his calling as a mail carrier. He can hear the mail truck when it enters the street. "Mail truck's here," he says. "In five minutes, it will be here." He literally timed it. Then he stands at the window and watches. When the mail comes, I bring it to him and make sure he has a letter opener. Something about that is deeply satisfying to him.

As for milk shakes, Grandma is against them. She thinks it makes him gain weight. (Although she gives him a big bowl of ice cream at 11 o'clock every night.) So I conveniently forget her complaints about this occasional afternoon treat. After all, this is about his happiness and well-being. Since a milk shake makes his day, I buy them once or twice a week.

At dinner time, I ask him questions that will lead to his stories. When I first lived with him, I got tired of hearing the same stories over and over again. It felt like torture. Then I realized how important it was to him. Grandpa would lean back in his chair, fold his arms, hold a toothpick between his teeth and smile widely as he began a tale. When I stopped to listen, I sometimes learned new details of the stories. Now, I've learned to enjoy those times. It's a beautiful thing.

Grandpa likes to watch sports on TV. He always has enjoyed sports. Now sports are more important than ever because he doesn't have to be able to hear the announcers to know what's happening. The hearing impairment doesn't interfere.

So I make it my business to know when games are going to be on TV. I either check the schedule every day, or I ask him to tell me which games are on and when they start. When I ask him, it gives him power to give me information. He is informing me. That's a beautiful thing.

Later in the day, when the game starts, I join him in the living room to make sure we get the game on TV. Sometimes he loses track of time or doesn't know which channel to use. If I have time, I sit and watch some of it with him, so he's not alone. I do not know for sure, but I think he really likes to have someone sit and watch TV with him. After all, who wants to sit alone all day?

I am a focused person. If I am watching TV, it's difficult for me to stop and talk with others. So I've had to train myself to break that habit with Grandpa. If we are watching TV and he wants to tell me a story, I stop watching, turn to face him, and listen to what he has to say. That's a part of communicating love and respect. And I get to enjoy whatever story he wants to tell me, even if I've heard it before.

To Each Her Own

What about Grandma's quality of life? That woman is like a hummingbird—always moving around. While Grandpa can sit in his chair most of the day, she does not want to stop for anything. It's almost compulsive. If she doesn't have one project going, she's got three she's trying to get done all at the same time! She can wear me out.

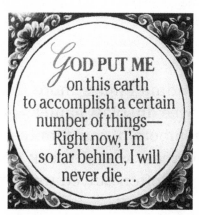

Grandma's refrigerator magnet.

GOD PUT ME on this earth to accomplish a certain number of things— Right now, I'm so far behind, I will never die...

At the beginning of the day, she has an agenda. She lies in bed thinking about it before she ever gets up. Just like me, she is an overly-ambitious, time optimist—we think we have all the time in the world! You'd think we'd learn otherwise when we don't get everything done, day after day!

I used to think that my doing some of those chores for Grandma would improve her quality of life. Was I ever wrong!

Here's what I found, to my great dismay: if I did all the laundry so that she didn't have to, she'd find something else to do. Often it was something more complicated and dangerous, like removing a tree from the yard. (No joke!)

You know what Grandma wants? She wants to keep doing things and feeling like she's getting things done. That helps her enjoy life. Sometimes she needs assistance doing those things. That's where I come in.

Sometimes it's frustrating. Why does she want to make a double batch of muffins at midnight? Can I get her to wait until tomorrow? No. So, I place the heavy flour and sugar containers on the counter, and stir the thick mixture when it's time.

So, contrary to general opinion, Grandma does not want to retire from being busy. In fact, she is afraid that if she sits too long, she may never get up. Hence, the compulsiveness.

Playing Games

There is one thing that Grandma enjoys more than anything, it seems. She loves to play games. For decades, when any four members of our family got together, a card game of Pinochle would break out. Being a competitive family, we often stayed up until 2 a.m. playing games.

Sometimes I hear Grandma call out from another room, "Does anyone want to play a game?"

Playing games is a great way to slow down when she's trying to do too much. It helps her sit down for a couple of hours and pace her day better. The benefits go on. Grandpa enjoys games too. Playing games helps keep everyone's minds sharper. Ultimately, their quality of life and enjoyment of the day is improved.

When Grandpa was hospitalized for two weeks, we put our chairs around the hospital bed, placed his eating table in the middle, and played a few hands of cards. We all had great fun!

Enlisting Others

There were times, especially on days when I was the sole caregiver, that I didn't have the time or energy to provide those extras on a regular basis. Sometimes I could sacrifice something else, like vacuuming, to squeeze in an activity.

When I couldn't be that person, I looked for visitors to help with those things. Sometimes they didn't like it, because I didn't communicate well enough. They were functioning as a quality-of-life enhancer, just by taking Grandma to the store, even though it seemed like a chore.

Or why did I suggest they play games with Grandpa and Grandma, while I'm away in my room? At those moments, they were enhancing Grandpa and Grandma's life, and giving a break to the caregiver. It doesn't seem like a glorious thing. Yet it was a bigger blessing than they know. Sometimes that's what being family is all about.

Out of House

What will quality of life look like for someone who is in a care facility or assisted-living residence? Let's look at that.

Many care facilities build in programs to enhance enjoyment through various activities such as Bingo, bowling, holiday parties, crafts, and more. I have seen some great successes in program activities. I really appreciate the people who work hard to provide fun and enjoyment in those homes.

Nothing, and I mean nothing, can take the place of knowing we are valued and feeling loved. I have seen some of the workers in those facilities communicate genuine care and love to the residents. I have seen residents who come to receive that love and care, and really rely on those workers for daily support and encouragement.

No matter how wonderful those workers are, they cannot entirely replace outside family and friends. Those workers are paid to be there. There is a difference in having a paid visitor and a voluntary visitor. Plus, the paid visitor may move on to take another job, meaning another loss in the life of that resident. But family doesn't change.

Regular time together says, "I love you.
You are important to me."

Feeling forgotten is far worse than losing your home or independence. It's worse than being served food you don't like and not getting outside every day. Too many of our loved ones experience the grief of being forgotten at the end of life. How do we know we are forgotten? When no one comes to see us. When children don't call on our birthday or on important holidays.

Quality of life for someone in a care facility or hospital is similar to caring for someone at home. It can be as simple as sitting with them for 2–3 hours (not 20 minutes).

Perhaps it means taking them outside for a walk, or to your home for a meal. Maybe it's bringing their favorite snack, or playing a game, or recounting favorite memories, or watching TV together.

Some of these beautiful people will object and say, "I know you're busy. Don't stop living life for me!" Don't believe it for a second! Yes, they love you. No, they don't want to inconvenience you. But, yes, they want to see you! Go to them.

Painful Visits

Maybe the situation is the exact opposite. Your parent or loved one hates being there and blames you. They demand that you give them all of your attention. They make visits nearly unbearable, constantly complaining, and saying, "Get me out of here!"

Grandma and I visited her friend Nina for two years, after Nina hurt her leg and the state placed her in a care facility. Nina always cried and complained when we visited. Sometimes it was difficult and unpleasant. But she also smiled and thanked us for coming. Her face would light up when we brought a soda or candy. One time, her sister, who lived three hours away, came to visit on her birthday. Otherwise, we were her only visitors. We continued to visit until she left for heaven.

If someone is difficult to be around, it's hard to visit. Yet they need love too. They may need it more than ever before. Sometimes I felt a moment of dread when I went to see Nina. I sat in the parking lot, gathering courage to walk in the facility. Yet, I almost always left feeling glad that I visited.

It's difficult to act nice when your life is coming to a close and you can't even do it in your own home. Oftentimes, physical pain causes people to act more mean and ornery. That can happen inside a care facility or in our own home. Pain may be the hidden cause of some of the outward anger people display when they are in a care home.

This does not excuse an abusive person. If the person you are caring for has a history of abusiveness, that is a different situation, and different guidelines apply for visits.

Wrap-up
This chapter came out of the later stages of caring for my grandparents, rather than the beginning, because they maintained so much independence initially. However, quality of life issues can occur at any time, such as with an extended hospital stay, with a stroke or debilitating illness, or when a person we care for moves to a new place. Moving to a new place requires a lot of adjustments, and aging or not, it takes time to build new patterns and routines that keep life interesting. We need to keep quality of life on the agenda for those we care for.

Also remember that we deserve quality in life too. The next chapter, about sanity, touches on that briefly. Many other wonderful books focus on caring for the caregiver, reminding us that we deserve to take care of ourselves also, and elaborate on ways to do that. My personal favorite is *The Selfish Pig's Guide to Caring* by Hugh Marriott.

Remembering our elderly loved ones, spending time with them, and finding ways to enhance their quality of life is a beautiful thing. Thank you for all you do to make life fulfilling for them!

Chapter 9

Sanity

"There is a fifth dimension beyond that which is known to man. It is a dimension as vast as space and as timeless as infinity. It is the middle ground between light and shadow, between science and superstition, and it lies between the pit of man's fears and the summit of his knowledge. This is the dimension of imagination. It is an area which we call the Twilight Zone."[7]

It's Real

I'd like to place a sign over the door to the house that reads, "You have now entered the Twilight Zone." It helps to enter this house with the clear understanding that logic and common-sense do not operate effectively in this realm. It's as if we live near a giant black hole that sucks all logic and reasoning ability away.

Many times people ask me to give examples when I tell them that Grandma sometimes acts crazy. At those moments my brain fails me and I find no examples, perpetuating an uneasy feeling that perhaps I am the one who truly doesn't know what's going on. I fail to remember that day one winter past when I arose in the morning, went to the kitchen to get a cup of coffee, and found the oven turned on with the door wide open, with nothing inside, and everyone else in bed.

Later, when I asked Grandma about it, she said the heater wasn't warming the house sufficiently, so she decided to use the oven also. She acted like it was no big deal, and thought I was out of line asking her not to do that. Grandpa heard us talking and asked what the fuss was all about. I told him, thinking he would take my side. He did not.

Those are the kinds of moments when I feel that I am living with people who are not entirely in their right minds. Those are the moments when I feel my own sanity beginning to slip, by the very nature of living in a world that doesn't make sense to me.

Working within Someone Else's Reality

Even now, Grandpa tells people, "I can still drive. But people would be angry if I got in an accident because of my bad eye."

It's tempting to disagree with him. However, it wouldn't help anyone. As long as he doesn't get behind the wheel again, he can stick with that story. My interjection would only hurt his dignity and make me a jerk. (Not to mention that he is right: he actually can turn on the car and make it go. He can drive, even if it's not safe.)

Every day there are instances where my perception of reality differs from theirs. Then I have to make a choice: insert my reality, or work within their reality. After many attempts to convert them to

110

my reality, I've generally found it less frustrating to work within theirs.

When these differences surface, it's okay to discuss different viewpoints and negotiate what to do. If they feel strongly about something, then we have to decide what to do—we decide who's choice to act on.

This is terribly frustrating when their perception does not match up with reality. For example, when Grandma wants to buy a certain item that no longer exists, and yet insists on visiting stores to look for it. I know we are looking for an obsolete item. Yet, I have to drive her around, and I have to ask the clerk to find the item, knowing all along it's not there, since Grandma can't verbalize her ideas as well anymore.

If I were an emotionless robot, this would be easy. Instead, I'm operating in her reality, which I know doesn't match up with today's reality. It feels futile. Those are moments when it's harder to maintain personal sanity. Especially, when we drive to the next store on the same fruitless mission. (When she learns the item is not there, she concludes that it's so popular it sold out.)

Nonetheless, as a general rule of thumb, choosing to operate in their reality is often the most helpful thing I can do in the quest to help them finish well. It shows respect. It doesn't ask them to change, especially when they don't want to change or can't conceive changing.

This is true even when someone is hallucinating, which has happened a couple of times as Alzheimer's disease progresses in Grandpa. It doesn't mean that

I'm required to confirm his perception, for example, that there is a bird in the room (when there is not). It means not shouting at him, "There's no bird in here!" Instead I can reassure him that it's going to be okay. Or I can open the door for a minute so the theoretical bird can fly out. After all, it's not theoretical to him.

Finding Ways to Keep Personal Sanity

One or two frustrating experiences from time to time doesn't send me over the edge. It's the repeated day-after-day insanities that build up like a steam cooker and begin to tear me down. When it happens day after day, multiple times each day, it brings me to the end of my rope.

If you are a full-time caregiver who has not felt extended frustration or burnout, or your own sense of sanity slipping at times, I am happy for you! You must be doing something right to take care of yourself. Perhaps you have an exceptionally good attitude.

The longer we care for others, the more we are at risk for physical, mental, and emotional health issues ourselves. We must build systems to take care of ourselves too. Next are some ways I find helpful.

Hit the Road (No Guilt Trips)

When I lose patience and become angry over small things, it tells me that I am not able to handle it anymore.

Then I let my family members know that I need to get away and we make arrangements. I leave town for two or three days. I make myself stop thinking about my grandparents and just live for myself on those days.

I know I need a break when I act snappy, not happy.

Things happen when I'm away from their house: I have "normal" interactions with others; I do things I enjoy; I have extended time to work on my projects without interruptions for emergencies; I do things my way instead of someone else's way. I don't think about these things consciously, but in doing them, I remember what I call "normal" life. It gives me hope that I can have that kind of life again when this season of caregiving ends.

That time away allows me to be refreshed inside. When I return home, I feel the difference and act appropriately with my grandparents. I need a break like that about once a month. The longer I go without a break like that, the longer break I need to reset my mind.

Once when my brother was living here, he began to snap at Grandma and get frustrated. I told him to go away for a few days so he could get a break. He replied, "I would, but I'm afraid if I go away, I won't come back." Sometimes he made powerful, true statements.

Since then, I have experienced that same sentiment a couple of times. It's not that I don't love my grandparents. It's just that I'm not always sure I can keep living in this situation without losing part of my mind too.

Such breaks are essential to the life and health of caregivers. Make every effort to get away from the home for more than 24 hours at regular intervals.

Exercise and Get Out of the House

Getting out of town once a month is not really enough to take care of myself and maintain my sense of personal sanity. I function best when I get out of the house at least once a day. That is easier said than done, especially for solitary caregivers. The irony is, when I am caregiving all by myself, I need it even more!

Each of us can find a way to do it. Some caregivers report that even going out by themselves shopping for groceries or picking up medications is a time that they feel like they can have for themselves. (I know it's time to take a break when running errands feels like a break.)

When I was alone, I made a point of walking in the morning before my grandparents woke up. In that way, I had time for myself, without leaving them at much risk. It was the best thing I did for myself!

Classes and Groups

The next best thing I did was attend classes and meetings about caregiving. I connected with others who understood. Suddenly I wasn't alone in my experiences. When someone said she was getting upset because her mother kept a wad of dollar bills that she counted again and again all day long, we nodded in understanding. I gained insight into the disease of dementia, making it easier for me to deal with the insanities at home.

Outside Life

Another way to maintain sanity is having a life outside the caregiving environment. For me that happens when I visit friends outside the home. Going to church can provide that outlet, as well as any club or recreational activity. It's a connection with non-dementia life that helps.

Tag-Team Care

Probably this goes without saying, but to be sure, "Enlist help from others!" I know it's not possible in every case. Where it's possible, ask for help. Establish a pattern as early as possible when care begins.

I know someone who uses her two week vacation every year to go home and give their siblings a break in caring for mom and dad. That's a difference maker!

Another friend was frustrated and burned out after caring for her mom for four years. None of her seven siblings offered to take over. She had to move out to make them step up to the plate.

Some of the Challenges

The rather bizarre, paradoxical situation a caregiver finds themselves in is this:

The better you care for a person, the longer they will live. The longer they live, the more care they will need to sustain daily life, making less personal down time for the carer, putting the carer at significantly greater risk for mental and physical health problems. Simply put, the better I care for a dementia patient, the worse my health may become.[8]

Here are just a few facts from the article "Caregiver Health"[9] by the Family Caregiver Alliance (caregiver.org):

- A substantial body of research shows that family members who provide care to individuals with chronic or disabling conditions are themselves at risk. Emotional, mental, and physical health problems arise from complex caregiving situations and the strains of caring for frail or disabled relatives.

- Nearly three quarters (72%) of caregivers reported that they had not gone to the doctor as often as they should, and more than half (55%) had missed doctor appointments.

- Estimates show that between 40 to 70% of caregivers have clinically significant symptoms of depression, with approximately one quarter to one half of these caregivers meeting the diagnostic criteria for major depression. Both caregiver depression and perceived burden increase as the care receiver's functional status declines.

- According to one study, there is a dramatic increase in risk of mental health consequences among women who provide 36 or more hours per week of care to a spouse.

- Caregivers suffer from increased rates of physical ailments (including acid reflux, headaches, and pain/aching), increased tendency to develop serious illness, and have high levels of obesity and bodily pain.

In contrast, one third of carers did not feel stress or negative effects. They report benefits to giving care.[10]

> Even when caregiving demands become more intense and result in high levels of distress and depression, caregivers often cite positive aspects of the experience. They report that caregiving makes them feel good about themselves and as if they are needed, gives meaning to their lives, enables them to learn new skills, and strengthens their relationships with others.[11]

Self-Care

An Alzheimer's Association class provided statistics about how caregiver health diminishes. It opened my eyes and made me determined not to become another statistic. Since I'd previously worked in another service field, I was familiar with the concept of good "self-care." People in service fields and those inclined to go out of their way to help others often need to learn how to take care of themselves. It's too easy to focus on others and forget about ourselves.

Some people are so busy taking care of others, and so sensitive to the needs of those around them, they actually feel guilty about taking care of themselves. In addition to logistical challenges, guilt often prevents caregivers from taking care of themselves—like new parents going out to dinner for the first time without the baby, who can't enjoy the evening because they can't stop thinking about the baby.

After five years of progressively involved caregiving, and entering middle-stage dementias, I saw the wear and tear on myself. That is why I have to stay committed to caring for myself. You have to care for yourself also! That's why so many books about caregiving actually focus on helping the caregiver take care of themselves rather than how to give care.

How is it that I spend two hours paying my grandparents bills and balancing their checkbook, and only give 20 minutes to take care of my finances? Have you heard of the Golden Rule? "Do to others as you would have them do to you."[12] It's a great rule. And I'm guessing that you are doing all that and more in the care you give to your loved one. Some of us need to practice the opposite rule: do for ourselves what we do for others. Did I take my grandpa to get his teeth cleaned, and fail to have my own teeth cleaned this year?

Do we believe in sacrificially caring for others? Absolutely. Then why put so much focus on caring for ourselves? The simple fact is this: if we don't take proper care of ourselves, we will burn out—then we will not be able to continue caring for others. That would be extremely counter-productive!

Not caring for ourselves is like buying a car and never taking time to get an oil change. Instead of lasting 10–20 years, we may only get 5 years out of the car. It doesn't make sense to take short cuts like that. The fact is you are worth taking care of. And you really need to put that on your list of things to do.

The "Why?" Question

Returning briefly to the paradox (that the better we care, the longer our loved one lives, and the worse our health becomes), caring for others becomes an opportunity for the dreaded *why* to invade our life. We have many opportunities in life to ask *"Why?"* Difficult, painful, and tragic times naturally bring it on. It often walks together with "I can't take it anymore"—those times when we feel we can't go on.

There was a point in caring for Grandpa, at the end, when I didn't know how our family would make it through the week. None of us could handle the violent outbursts that began taking place. We couldn't restrain him from hurting himself or coming after us. We were not equipped to protect ourselves from physical violence.

Where were the answers at that moment? What could we do? Place him in a special facility? That would've tormented both him and us, even though it was the only option left. It was a high-stakes lose-lose picture.

The same week that dilemma arose, he stopped eating and drinking. He stopped responding to people. The progress of Alzheimer's disease had eroded his mind. And he didn't have much left to live for.

When his body began to shut down, we didn't have to face any more violent outbursts. Instead we walked with him through the "valley of the shadow of death." He was dying before our eyes. So a new torment, questions, and deep sadness pressed against our souls, as we ministered to him in his dying days.

"Why is this happening?" It's the deep existential question we ask, especially in our darkest times. It's nearly inescapable. And there is rarely a satisfactory answer.

"Why would God allow this?" Another of the big *why* questions many of us ask. Some people even stop believing in God or refuse to believe in God because of painful situations. We can't fathom how a loving God who would allow such pain and unnecessary suffering.[13]

There will be days when the *whys* and the suffering enigmas that birth that question play with our minds and challenge our sanity. We find a way to continue stepping out each day.

After a struggle with *why?* I eventually find peace in knowing that it's okay not to have an answer to everything. I commit to give love. Love overcomes a multitude of wrongs.

This leads to another practice related to sanity and survival.

Prayer

God is our refuge and our strength, an ever-present help in trouble.[14]

> About 73% of surveyed caregivers said praying
> helps them cope with caregiving stress.[15]

I turn to God every day for help. I tell him my concerns. I ask for grace that I will be loving and do right for my grandparents. I ask for his peace upon them. I ask for his protection.

God has protected Grandma from many falls. Praise God! God made it possible for Grandpa to stay home and pass away at home, surrounded by loved ones. That was an answered prayer. God brought me to live with my grandparents to help them in the last stages of life. God brought my parents to help me and my grandparents. God provided good doctors. The list goes on and on.

Even if you aren't sure God exists, you can pray. It doesn't cost money. If you're not sure how to pray, some sample prayers are available at the end of this book.

I ask others to pray for me. It still amazes me how quickly relief comes to my soul when others pray for me. It shouldn't surprise me. I think, "Why didn't I ask sooner?!" (Another *why* question.)

Recognizing and Avoiding Elder Abuse

I can understand how some elder abuse happens. Here are adults, grown human beings, who are sometimes so out of touch with reality that they cause serious or dangerous errors, to themselves and others—and they can't be controlled or stopped. Some attempts at control turn into abuse.

Voice Control

Even people with good intentions can become seeming monsters when sanity gets lost in the mix. Have you ever been around a person who is insane, or out of touch with reality? It is difficult to remain sane and have meaningful communication with that person—not impossible, but very difficult.

It's hard to see clearly when we are close to it. It's difficult to stop from yelling or trying to assert control in out-of-control situations. Once I tried yelling at Grandma so I wouldn't have to physically stop her from recklessly pushing a loaded, heavy wheel barrel across the bumpy lawn.

That measured attempt to use my voice to assert control didn't work, and didn't feel right, so I didn't do it again. There have been times when I unknowingly, unwittingly raised my voice or spoke in an angry tone, only to realize later what I'd done.

Those were hard moments to look at and digest. I'm grateful that somehow, someway, I reflected on those moments and recognized the ugliness in me. When I did, I went to Grandma and apologized. (It was usually Grandma who prompted extreme frustration in me.) She was always gracious about it.

In recognizing that I was capable of speaking that way, and not liking it, I was able to make a gradual change and stop using anger in attempts to control Grandma's behaviors. It's helped me be a better person, and made it easier for her to have me around. I'm less inclined to do or say things I'll regret later.

That angry way of handling frustrating situations runs in my family, because I've seen others do it also. That is how Grandpa would respond to Grandma when she had an outlandish plan. I guess she specializes in unusual solutions, like using a bungee cord to hold the toilet seat up. (Not just any bungee cord, a special one that can't be found in stores.) Like using Gorilla Glue to keep the carpet from fraying. Like using White Out to paint the door frame. Like using the oven to heat the house.

Even though yelling was the family pattern, it wasn't acceptable behavior from me. Grandpa was the only one allowed to raise his voice at her. He'd been doing it for 70 years. And she'd promptly yell back.

Step Back

Reflect on your way of handling a frustrating situation. Did you handle it in a way that was respectful? Would an outsider consider your response appropriate?

If you find that you need help dealing with the frustrations and avoiding abusive patterns, step back and get help. Caregiver stress is one of the common reasons abuse (and neglect) occurs, especially for those caring for someone with a mental illness, such as dementia.

It can happen with any caregiver, whether male or female, and by a spouse or family member or outside caregiver. If it occurs, it's time to seek help from a counselor or support group and appoint someone else to help for a time.

The best approach is prevention—getting respite care to reduce stress. Respite care means someone else comes to help out while you get a day or weekend break. Some city and county governments provide free respite care so caregivers can get a much needed break. Reducing stress is one key to preventing an abusive situation as you provide care.

Be Kind to Yourself

Yes, there will be days when you want to cry, scream, drink till you don't think, or eat a tub of ice cream to cope with the stress. Give yourself a pass to have a bad day (or week). Then start practicing healthy routines to cope with stress. Laughter always helps, and it's no coincidence that *stressed* spelled backwards is *desserts*.

Sanity is a wonderful thing. Make every effort to preserve it. It benefits you and all those around you. Taking proactive steps to take care of yourself will help maintain sanity, even as you enter the Twilight Zone.

Chapter 10

Logistics

Complicated (adj.) 1. The best word to describe managing someone else's business as their life nears the finish line.

The Moment It Counts

It happens when we sit in a doctor office, needing to fill out 15 pages of detailed medical history, insurance forms, and more. Grandma writes painfully slow and writing is painful in her arthritic hands. This could take an hour, I thought. So I fill out the forms, as I read each question to her in the waiting room.

It happens when the ambulance arrives and they need to know *stat* what medications she is taking and if she is allergic to any meds. It happens when, arriving at the hospital ER, they want to know if she has filled out papers for end-of-life preferences, such as whether to resuscitate if she stops breathing. (That's the infamous DNR, or Do Not Resuscitate form.)

There are a number of things we can get in place that make life easier before things get complicated. Just getting these things in place is a complicated process, but every item taken care of before the critical point saves headaches and roadblocks later. You only find out how critical it is when a doctor in the ER is in front of you, asking if they can use penicillin (and you don't remember), or asking who has authority to determine whether they should resuscitate if your loved one's heart stops during a procedure. You need the answer before that moment arrives.

Five Musts

1. List of Medications

We keep a list of medications, supplements (vitamins, etc.), allergies, and major health issues on a single sheet of paper, updating it with changes along the way. We bring it to doctor visits, so we don't have to rely on memory. We have one printed in the house to hand to medical professionals in emergencies. We use it to fill the pill box each week. We use it to make sure prescription medications are filled regularly. It helps prevent mistakes and gives critical information to first responders in an emergency. (See example at the end of book.)

2. Health Directives

This is a must for all of us, not only our elders. Look online for forms to fill out. This tells the doctors whether or not to use life support, and more. It takes pressure off of family members and helps avoid family arguments about what's best for the loved one.

3. Power of Attorney

This may not be possible in every situation. However, it's a must when it is possible. Don't wait until after a stroke, when it may not be possible to get critical papers set up. Don't wait until dementia renders your loved one unable to appoint a trusted family member to manage affairs. Read up online about power of attorney. Speak with an attorney if you can afford it. If not, it's possible to print and sign a generic one.

4. Add Your Name to Every List—HIPAA Clearance

HIPAA (pronounced "hip-uh") means Health Insurance Portability and Accountability Act (of 1996). See www.hhs.gov/hipaa for exhaustive information. HIPAA defines standards for health care providers about what information they can and can't share about patients. In some cases, without prior permission, a family member can't receive or access information about health care.

Over time, we began to set permissions with doctors and providers so I could call to order a prescription refill and resolve unfilled prescriptions. When the doctors call to give a test result, I can get the information and relay it to Grandma, because she doesn't hear well and often can't remember all that was said.

Yes, with power of attorney, I can arrange to do all those things. However, even with power of attorney, it works much better to have the person you are caring for arrange the authorization.

When Grandpa couldn't manage calling to resolve problems with the cable provider, I helped him with the phone calls. The cable company needed verbal permission from Grandpa to allow me to authorize changes and discussions. From the cable company to credit card companies to the pharmacy filling prescriptions, my name is on each company's list, so I can act in their behalf.

5. *Name on the bank account*

We didn't need this at first. Then Grandpa couldn't do the bills anymore. One day he sat at the table for five hours, looking at the same papers again and again, and still couldn't figure them out. Later his hand started shaking, so that he couldn't write well. So I filled out the bills and checks and Grandma signed them. A year later, Grandma's hands are hurting so that she doesn't want to sign the checks anymore. She would rather not bother thinking about them. We also recognize that having another person who can handle bills is crucial, because if Grandma is hospitalized, someone still needs to pay the electric bill. Or, if Grandma goes to heaven before Grandpa, we need a way to care for him. Truth be told, I didn't want my name on the account, because in some families the person with the name on the account is the one other family members look at suspiciously after all is said and done. But until that time, my grandparents need help. Another option is setting up electronic payments online.

Helpful Extras

- Keep a list of doctors and their phone numbers posted by the home phone. It makes it easier to schedule an appointment with specialists, such as the dermatologist, to check that new growth on Grandpa's head. By making it visible, the list is available to everyone who helps out.

- Keep a list of family members and phone numbers posted by the home phone or in easy reach. I know, it's old-school. Yet Grandma could call people and stay in touch without having to ask me for help. It's easy to call a relative from the home phone. If there is an emergency and we want to call family members to let them know what's going on, the printed phone list facilitates it. If a friend or neighbor is visiting, and there is an emergency, they will have someone to contact (if they don't have your number in their cell phone).

- Keep a record or log of doctor visits and medical procedures and surgeries by year. Grandpa began creating a log years ago. His log is 15 pages long. We can easily look and see that his last colonoscopy was five years ago. We can see that when he last had anesthesia, his heartbeat became erratic. The doctor uses this information when he considers the level of risk for the next procedure.

- If you are caring for an American Veteran of War, you'll need their DD214 document to access services and benefits available to war veterans.

Chapter 11

Organizations That Help

There are many organizations to help as you step into the caregiving role. The more you tap into these resources and support organizations, the better off you will be! Some groups and services are locally organized. A few national ones are highlighted here. No one paid for endorsement in this book. They have simply helped me and my family through this time of life. Every time we reach out, it helps more than we imagined.

The Alzheimer's Association

www.alz.org

This non-profit organization is the cream-of-the-crop in my opinion. I'm grateful for the way they have trained and supported my family.

Dementia occurs when the brain begins to atrophy, or deteriorate. Alzheimer's disease is one form of several types of dementia.

The organization provided classes that educated my family about all aspects of caregiving, from understanding the disease itself, recognizing the need to take care of ourselves as caregivers, and finding strategies to give the best care to our loved ones.

They also coordinate support groups. Some groups were better than others. Keep looking around until you find a group that works well for you. Give it a chance to work.

I found that the seminars and classes mimicked some benefits of a support group: I felt understood; I found that I wasn't alone; I wasn't the only one dealing with these challenges; I wasn't the only one who felt sanity slipping away at times; I found new ideas for making home life better; I found new understanding for what was happening, such as why Grandpa didn't like to leave the house so much anymore. Suddenly it made sense that he was feeling depressed. Suddenly I learned that there does come a time when Grandma shouldn't be using sharp knives in the kitchen anymore, and it's okay for me to be the one making that decision. What a relief I felt!

I learned the importance of educating myself. I learned that the rest of my family also needs to be educated about the disease. I don't have to be the primary teacher. I could simply ask those family members involved in giving care to my grandparents to attend a seminar or two.

The Alzheimer's Association has offices around the country, plus great online resources, for those who can't leave home easily. Every Alzheimer's Association office is run by different people. I found the representatives to be compassionate and well-informed.

Meals on Wheels

www.mealsonwheelsamerica.org

While we did not need the services of Meals on Wheels, it's the ideal service for families who do not live near their aging loved one. There came a point when Grandma could no longer cook all the meals. Had a family member not lived with her, we would have called Meals on Wheels for help.

They deliver a healthy meals to elders. At the same time, your loved one sees a friendly face. And someone knows that your loved one is home and able to answer the door. I have an elderly neighbor who lives all alone. I am concerned that she could fall or have a stroke and no one would know about it for days. She dismisses my concern. Meals on Wheels volunteers know when the door isn't answered and can alert someone that something may be amiss.

An excerpt from their website states:

> Millions of American families sleep better at night and can continue their daily routines and responsibilities because they know that Meals on Wheels is keeping a watchful eye over their aging loved ones. When other competing responsibilities make it impossible or difficult for us to be there, Meals on Wheels can make sure our parents, grandparents and others important in our lives are cared for, and that someone is there to raise a red flag if something doesn't seem just right.[16]

Family Caregiver Alliance

www.caregiver.org
www.caregiver.org/family-care-navigator
800-445-8106

The Family Care Navigator is the go-to place for state-specific information on services in the United States. This is a big step forward, because it used to be a major research process to understand what services are available. For example, my uncle wondered why I hadn't applied to California state for supplemental income for caregiving. When I looked into it several years ago, I couldn't even find who to call or ask if California had such a plan. The Family Care Navigator now sets this information out, state by state.

The Family Caregiver Alliance website provides training and support group resources, plus an 800 number so caregivers can speak to a real person (not a machine) for help in assessing needs and service referrals. I love that FCA addresses a broad range of care situations, including care for adults with chronic physical or cognitive conditions such as stroke, Parkinson's, and other illnesses.

CareGiving.com

Started by an individual carer, CareGiving.com offers resources and support for the caregiver. It offers a personal touch, and allows carers to be involved at various levels. I especially appreciate that they offer many online forums that allow caregivers in remote locations to be connected to a supportive community. This site is a must-visit for caregivers.

Hospice Foundation of America

www.hospicefoundation.org

At one of the hardest moments in life, hospice care workers and volunteers walk with us and our loved one who about to transition out of this world.

In the midst of writing this book, Grandpa's health declined considerably. After a week-long hospital visit, and a month in a nursing home, he was able to return home. However, his motivation for living dwindled and Alzheimer's disease marched on.

One day, Grandpa stopped eating and drinking, and became unresponsive. The family wanted to know what to do. Take Grandpa to the hospital?

The hospital wasn't the answer this time. If possible, he would not spend his last days hooked up to monitors in a hospital gown in an unfamiliar room. I knew about hospice care from a neighbor who received care at the end of her days. We called the Hospice Foundation of America. Professionals visited and determined he was in his final days.

We gratefully accepted their service. They instructed us on how to care for Grandpa. Nurses came by every day. Aids came to help with bathing. They supplied a hospital bed and supplies. Help was only a phone call away. When the time came, I administered morphine to him, to ease the pain as his body shut down. Probably one of the hardest weeks of my life. Yet, he remained at home, as he had wanted.

Hospice volunteers also came by to assist our family in the grief process. They were vital in helping Grandma to say goodbye. We didn't know how to help her.

Become familiar with hospice care in your area. The Hospice Foundation of America has an online directory, with contact information for each state or region.

Administration for Community Living

www.acl.gov/programs

The Administration for Community Living (ACL) is another provider of information on local resources, by zip code and city name, via the Eldercare Locator (www.eldercare.gov). The ACL advocates that people stay in community-based care of their choice. They offer insight, research, and resources to promote that goal.

> "ACL believes that home- and community-based services and supports should be robust enough that individuals with even the most complex medical and behavioral needs can be appropriately and effectively supported in their own home or other community-based settings."

AARP

www.aarp.org

While not a traditional caregiving website, AARP provides valuable information for avoiding scams, help with financial planning, and navigating Medicare. They also offer a section dedicated to caregiving.

Alliance on Aging

allianceonaging.org

The local Monterey County agency for senior services. Ombudsman, tax assistance, Medicare counseling, and more are offered via Alliance on Aging. This organization sponsored the first workshop I attended about elder care, and it opened the door to my family journey.

That's a Wrap

You've made it to the official end of the book. Now you have some resources to help you and your loved ones finish well in this caregiving journey. It's rarely less than frightening, daring, perilous, quandry-filled, and enigmatic. Remember to slow down enough to enjoy the rewarding moments. In the hairiest of difficult times, know that your presence makes a difference. You may not be able to control the outcome, but you make life better for those you care for.

Beatrice's Story

From a Yahoo! news reporter:

> "It pays to be kind. Just ask Beatrice Gray of Australia. Ms. Gray had spent years helping out her elderly neighbor, Betty Harris. Well, when Ms. Harris died she left her entire $12.5 million estate to Ms. Gray. After two years of lawsuits from the Harris family, the Australian Supreme Court has decided Ms. Gray gets to keep the inheritance... I'm going to make sure the old guy next door has everything he needs."[17]

When I heard this story, I was not surprised. The character quality of Betty's blood relatives is a moot point. Picture the timeline in the life of an octogenarian.

THE MIDDLE YEARS

0 - 20 YEARS   60 - 80+

She spent the first twenty years of life growing up. The next forty or fifty years were likely consumed with family life—husband, children, grandchildren. The final ten to twenty years...alone. While those 40–50 years of family life were special, it occurred during her prime years. During those years, she was the provider, the giver, the one others sought for help.

Now life has changed. In the last ten to twenty years, in the later stages of life, she is in need. Those needs increase and grow every month, every year. Yet, her family members are not around. Who will help?

She may be fortunate enough to have a neighbor or friend notice her need and offer to help. That person helps in her time of need. Meanwhile she doesn't often see the family members that she loves and cares for. She probably covers up her needs when they visit (for a couple weekends each year). She doesn't want them to know she needs help. And even if they watch for it, they don't want to see it. They feel happy and relieved that "all seems well with Grandma."

We don't ask if she needs someone to mow the lawn. Or perhaps we mow it. Who mows it the 50 weeks of the year that we aren't around?

If the family is too busy to stop and help, then she gets left out more and more.

Life is VERY DIFFICULT for an aging person. It is not a surprise that some people leave their inheritance (willingly, not by scam) to the people who showed love and care in their time of greatest need.

This is not about helping our family members so that we deserve or receive an inheritance. It's helping because a fellow human is in need—someone from our circle of life. And when our day comes, we will need help also.

Preventing Elder Abuse

The first step in prevention is understanding. Different types of elder abuse to watch out for include physical abuse, sexual abuse, financial abuse, emotional and psychological abuse, and neglect. If you suspect abuse, it's important to act. Here are some resources for understanding, preventing, and reporting abuse.

National Center on Elder Abuse (NCEA)

www.ncea.acl.gov

Website description: The National Center on Elder Abuse, directed by the U.S. Administration on Aging, contains comprehensive information about all areas of elder abuse, including financial exploitation. The site allows you to find resources on a state-by-state basis and provides telephone numbers for reporting elder abuse for each state.

The National Adult Protective Services Association (NAPSA)

www.napsa-now.org

Website description: The National Adult Protective Services Association is a non-profit organization with members in all 50 states whose purpose is to provide Adult Protective Services programs with a forum to share information, solve problems, and improve the quality of services for victims of elder abuse.

Eldercare Locator

www.eldercare.gov

eldercare.acl.gov/public/resources/topic/Elder_Abuse.aspx

Website description: The Eldercare Locator is a public service of the U.S. Administration on Aging that helps connect older adults and their families to services and resources in their local area, including resources for those who have been victims of elder abuse. Individuals may call 1-800-677-1116. Spanish-speaking specialists and access to a 150-language line service are available. TTY/TTD users should access local relay service or dial 711. Instruct the Relay Operator to connect you to the Eldercare Locator at 1-800-677-1116.

National Committee for the Prevention of Elder Abuse (NCPEA)

www.preventelderabuse.org

Website description: The National Committee for the Prevention of Elder Abuse provides information on all aspects of elder abuse. The NCPEA Web site has a designated section to help victims and those vulnerable to abuse. It provides information on what to do if you suspect abuse, services to stop the abuse, and resources in your community.

Sample Caregiver's Prayer

Prayer connects us with God, the Creator of the universe. God knows all things and understands you. The Bible says, "Cast all your anxiety on him because he cares for you."[18]

God can handle our pain, our anger, our troubles. He comforts us in our time of need. He rescues us and provides for us. He gives us wisdom when we ask. Go to him as you would go to an all-powerful King or a loving parent.

The Serenity Prayer[19]

> God, grant me to the serenity to accept the
>   things I cannot change,
> Courage to change the things I can,
> And wisdom to know the difference.

"Popcorn" Prayer

In times of trouble, I simply call out, "God, help me!" God is always there to help.

Additional Prayer Resources

Some ministries offer prayer hotlines and prayer request forms available online. For example, Kenneth Copeland Ministries, www.kcm.org/real-help/prayer, 1-817-852-6000, and Andrew Womack ministries at www.awmi.net/contact-us.

Sample Personal Medications List

We kept an updated list of medications and conditions in our vehicle and purses. We also brought extra copies to doctors offices. It helped when filling out forms and updating prescription information.

FULL NAME
Birthdate 12/12/1901

PRESCRIPTION MEDICATIONS:

LEVOTHYROXINE – 75mcg 1x day, Dr. Kent
RESTASIS – 0.4 ml, 1 drop 2x day, both eyes, Dr. Au
EVISTA – 60mg, 1x per day, Dr. Gray
LOVAZA – 900 mg Omega-3, 4x day (since 1/2010)
NEXIUM – 40 mg, 1x day, Dr. Kent (digestion)
CYMBALTA – 30 mg, 1x day, Dr. Kent, shingles pain
EDARBI – 40 mg, 1x day, Dr. Clover, lower blood pressure (began 9/26/12)

NON-PRESCRIPTION MEDS & VITAMINS:

ASPIRIN – 81mg one/day
I CAP (AREDS) – 1x day
CO Q10 (Ubiquinone) – 200 mg day
Acidophilus Lactobacillin – two/bedtime
Cranberry Concentrate – 500mg, 2x day
Liquid Calcium – 2 tbsp day
Vitamin C – 500 mg day
Senokot-S – as needed

(updated 9/25/2012)

PHYSICAL CONDITIONS:

HEART ARRHYTHMIA

**MASSECTOMY Right breast –
USE LEFT ARM FOR BLOOD PRESSURE**

**CORNEAL TRANSPLANTS
Both Eyes**

NOTE: Consult doctor before taking aspirin due to transplants

ALLERGIC TO:
CODINE
IODINE - BETADINE
DOXYCYCLINE
HYDROCODONE
VICODIN
CIPROFLOXACIN
IBUPROFIN

Dr. Kent suggests ampicillin if antibiotic is needed.

10 Early Signs and Symptoms of Alzheimer's

1. Memory loss that disrupts daily life.

One of the most common signs of Alzheimer's, especially in the early stages, is forgetting recently learned information. Others include forgetting important dates or events; asking for the same information over and over; relying on memory aides (e.g., reminder notes or electronic devices) or family members for things they used to handle on their own.

What's typical? Sometimes forgetting names or appointments, but remembering them later.

2. Challenges in planning or solving problems.

Some people may experience changes in their ability to develop and follow a plan or work with numbers. They may have trouble following a familiar recipe or keeping track of monthly bills. They may have difficulty concentrating and take much longer to do things than they did before.

What's typical? Making occasional errors when balancing a checkbook.

3. Difficulty completing familiar tasks at home, at work or at leisure.

People with Alzheimer's often find it hard to complete daily tasks. Sometimes, people may have trouble driving to a familiar location, managing a budget at work or remembering the rules of a favorite game.

What's typical? Occasionally needing help to use the settings on a microwave or to record a television show.

4. Confusion with time or place.

People with Alzheimer's can lose track of dates, seasons and the passage of time. They may have trouble understanding something if it is not happening immediately. Sometimes they may forget where they are or how they got there.

What's typical? Getting confused about the day of the week but figuring it out later.

5. Trouble understanding visual images & spatial relationships.

For some people, having vision problems is a sign of Alzheimer's. They may have difficulty reading, judging distance and determining color or contrast. In terms of perception, they may pass a mirror and think someone else is in the room. They may not recognize their own reflection.

What's typical? Vision changes related to cataracts.

6. New problems with words in speaking or writing.

People with Alzheimer's may have trouble following or joining a conversation. They may stop in the middle of a conversation and have no idea how to continue or they may repeat themselves. They may struggle with vocabulary, have problems finding the right word or call things by the wrong name (e.g., calling a watch a "hand clock").

What's typical? Sometimes having trouble finding the right word.

7. Misplacing things and losing the ability to retrace steps.

A person with Alzheimer's disease may put things in unusual places. They may lose things and be unable to go back over their steps to find them again. Sometimes, they may accuse others of stealing. This may occur more frequently over time.

What's typical? Misplacing things from time to time, such as a pair of glasses or the remote control.

8. Decreased or poor judgment.

People with Alzheimer's may experience changes in judgment or decision making. For example, they may use poor judgment when dealing with money, giving large amounts to telemarketers. They may pay less attention to grooming or keeping themselves clean.

What's typical? Making a bad decision once in a while.

9. Withdrawal from work or social activities.

A person with Alzheimer's may start to remove themselves from hobbies, social activities, work projects or sports. They may have trouble keeping up with a favorite sports team or remembering how to complete a favorite hobby. They may also avoid being social because of the changes they have experienced.

What's typical? Sometimes feeling weary of work, family and social obligations.

10. Changes in mood and personality.

The mood and personalities of people with Alzheimer's can change. They can become confused, suspicious, depressed, fearful or anxious. They may be easily upset at home, at work, with friends or in places where they are out of their comfort zone.

What's a typical age-related change? Developing very specific ways of doing things and becoming irritable when a routine is disrupted.

Source: www.alz.org/alzheimers-dementia/10_signs. Used with permission.

Acknowledgments

My family has been a tremendous support! It may sometimes appear from my tales that I am the sole caregiver, but that is not the case. We have been truly blessed with an ideal situation, where no one person shoulders the burden of caring for my grandparents. Wayne, Ray, Margie, Danny, Mitch, and Vince have especially contributed to the total care of Grandpa and Grandma. It's been a family thing.

Never have I had to feel totally alone or without help. Thank God! I don't know many people with that much support. We all credit Grandpa and Grandma for being examples to us. Because of their example, they never had to ask the family to come help them. Ultimately, God deserves all the credit. As Grandma said, "I prayed that God would give us help. He brought you here to help us." God heard her request and provided. And God sustained me as a carer.

Endnotes

1. Alzheimer's Association, "factsheet," March 2012, https://www.alz.org/media/Documents/public-health-news-march-2012.pdf.

2. U.S. Administration on Aging, "A Talk with an Elder Driver," April 13, 2012, http://www.eldercare.gov/Eldercare.NET/Public/Resources/Factsheets/Talk_Elder_Driver.aspx, (accessed July 17, 2014). Also https://eldercare.acl.gov/Public/Resources/Factsheets/Talk_Elder_Driver.aspx.

3. From http://www.helpguide.org/articles/aging-well/age-and-driving-safety-tips.htm.

4. See http://www.techtimes.com/articles/67253/20150728/driverless-cars-safe.htm, and http://www.businessinsider.com/why-driverless-cars-will-be-safer-than-human-drivers-2016-11.

5. Fisher Center for Alzheimer's Research Foundation, https://www.alzinfo.org/articles/promoting-independence-alzheimers-care/. Emphasis added.

6. Florida Health Care Association, http://www.fhca.org/members/qi/clinadmin/dignity2.pdf. Long Term Care Community Coalition, https://ltcombudsman.ny.gov/Resources/2010VolunteerTrainings/LTCCLTCOPTrainingsPresentation2010.pdf.

7. Season 1 opening to the 1960's TV series "The Twilight Zone" classically delivered by Rod Sterling. Shows are available to view online.

8. Caveat: While this statement is supported by

statistics, it is not a certainty for everyone. This statement mainly applies to primary or full-time caregivers who give care more than four years.

9. Family Caregiver Alliance, "Caregiver Health," https://www.caregiver.org/caregiver-health, accessed May 27, 2017.

10. Richard Schulz, et al., "Health Effects of Caregiving: the Caregiver Health Effects Study: An Ancillary Study of the Cardiovascular Health Study," *Annals of Behavioral Medicine*, 1997, 19 (2): 110–6.

11. Ibid.; Richard Schulz and Paula R. Sherwood, "Physical and Mental Health Effects of Family Caregiving," *American Journal of Nursing*, Sep 2008, 108 (9 Suppl): 23–27, doi:10.1097/01. NAJ.0000336406.45248.4c.

12. From the Bible, Luke 6:31.

13. There are many books and sources that address the question "How could a loving God allow this kind of suffering?" (For example, *Walking with God through Pain and Suffering* by Timothy Keller.) I have asked the question myself more than once. And I have found answers that satisfied my search—answers that allowed me to believe that a good God exists and remains worthy of my allegiance. This same God suffered also, so that I could have a hope and a future. God helped me in my moments of greatest need.

14. Psalm 46:1.

15. National Alliance for Caregiving/AARP, Caregiving in the U.S., 2004, http://assets.aarp.org/ rgcenter/il/us_caregiving_1.pdf.

16. From www.mealsonwheelsamerica.org/theissue /problemandsolution.

17. From http://screen.yahoo.com/woman-leaves-12-5-million-000025084.html.

18. From the Bible, 1 Peter 5:7.

19. By American theologian Reinhold Niebuhr (1892–1971).

Made in the USA
Coppell, TX
25 October 2020